Nativitas xpi in bethlem iudae ... magi munera offerunt
et infantes interficiuntur ...

the CELTS

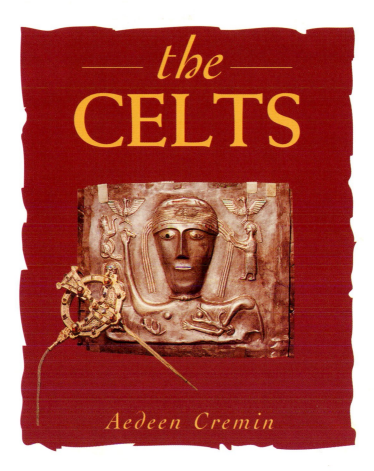

Aedeen Cremin

RIZZOLI
NEW YORK

Contents

Introduction 6

1. People of the West 8

2. Women of Spirit 24

3. Chiefs and Warriors 38

4. The Word is Law — the Druids 54

5. Encountering the Other — The Celt as Wanderer 70

6. *From Anarchy to Submission —
the Hammer of Rome 83*

7. *Beyond Rome — Freedom in the Celtic Fringe 96*

8. *Islands of Saints, Scholars and
Illuminated Manuscripts 112*

9. *Peoples of the Goddess and the Parallel
World of Faery 128*

10. *Fated Lovers 140*

*Further Reading 154
Index 156*

INTRODUCTION

T he Celts are a fascinating people, much misunderstood, sometimes maligned, sometimes exalted beyond their deserts. They prized liberty above security, loyalty above common sense, and beauty above all things. The beauty of a woman, of a man, of a landscape, of a fine object were celebrated in a myriad of ways, in song, poetry, feasting, and even in death.

This book can only be an invitation to enter the complex and still-mysterious world of the Celts. We know only fragments of their lives, enough to get the general outline of their history, but not enough to chart in detail all aspects of their thought. They would have preferred it that way, since they saw the everyday world as a shadow of that real world hidden from us by the routines of daily life.

This place some Celts called Avalon; others referred to it as the land of youth or the land belonging to the people of the goddess, and they prepared their entire lives for entry into that mystical and revered world. Today some Celts may call it the Christian heaven, and that too was known to their ancestors for whom there was but one God, manifest in all aspects of nature and human goodness.

This book deals with about 1500 years of Celtic culture from its beginnings around 500 BC to the start of its decline around AD 1100. It will follow the history of the Celtic world and bring out those aspects which make it different from the rest of Europe. We shall particularly notice its distinctive art styles, its social structures and the relationship between men and women within that structure. Celtic history will be quickly traced, or rather histories, for there are many Celtic worlds, all with individual features depending on their time and place but sharing a common culture and languages. Myths from Ireland and Britain will also be featured within these pages, highlighting the Celts' sense of passion and magic.

Despite all our research, the ancient Celts still elude us. Their culture most resembles one of those western islands, whose contours change, and may even vanish, in the misty light of the Atlantic seas.

People of the West

People of Romance

The Celts were a dramatic and romantic people. They were hardworking folk, but folk who looked beyond the daily cycle of drudgery to a world of infinite possibilities. The outward expression of their resilient optimism was a love of beautiful things, and music and stories in which men were strong, loyal and brave, but were enthralled by women whose passions defied convention. It was the Celts' historical misfortune to be surrounded by other people who thought that virtue lay in the middle path and who admired moderation, prudence and all those other sensible values by which most of us, even the Celts, have to live our lives.

Celtic culture was one of excess. Vanity was not reproached but considered normal and positively admirable, representing a proper sense of self-worth. Generosity was prized above all else. To be open-handed, not to count the cost, these were the marks of a true hero or heroine.

Next to generosity came wit. Words were a tool so powerful they could defeat an opponent on the field of battle, bring down a bad king, dismiss an unsatisfactory lover, overturn a poor judgement. The Celtic love of words has fortunately survived in a torrent of poetry and stories from early Britain and Ireland, which can vividly evoke for us that long lost time when the Celts were the most important people of western and central Europe.

The area of Celtic culture extended by the second century BC over most of western Europe, all of the Alps, much of the Danube valley and part of Turkey. Most of it was later incorporated into the Roman Empire. North of the Alps and Pyrenees was the area known as Celtica: Within this area most people spoke Gaulish, but in Spain another language, Celtiberian, was spoken. British and Pictish were spoken in Britain and Gaelic in Ireland.

❧ *Celtica* ❧

Strictly speaking, we should talk not about Celts, but about Celtic peoples, since there were about forty different groups united by language and cultural values. Though we have discovered a great deal about them, we are undoubtedly missing many significant details of lifestyle and history. Our knowledge of Celtic culture and values comes from a variety of sources: archeology, official Latin-language documents,

▼ *The Celts learnt to extract salt from the earth from about 1000 BC, enabling them to preserve meat and fish which kept them strong and healthy all year round. These saltmines in Hallstat, Austria are still worked today, underneath the buildings in the centre of the picture. The Celtic people lived on the narrow strip of land along the lake but were buried in the wooded area near the mines. The saltmines have served as a rich source of information about the Celts and their lifestyle; the graves provide a complete sequence of almost a thousand years of Celtic life and death.*

a huge variety of Celtic-language texts, and travellers' descriptions of Celtica — mainland Europe north of the Pyrenees.

The greatest Celtic period was in the two centuries 400–200 BC. During that time the Celtic peoples' territory stretched from northwestern Ireland to central Turkey in a great curving wedge which took in all of modern Britain, France, Belgium, Luxemburg, Switzerland, Austria, Slovenia, the Czech republic, Slovakia, Hungary and substantial parts of Portugal, Spain, Italy, the Netherlands, Germany, Serbia, Romania, Bulgaria and northwestern Turkey.

Celtic peoples continued to live in all of these places, but lost their languages and cultures as the various areas became incorporated into the Roman Empire from about 150 BC. In the end Celtic languages survived only in the British Isles and in Brittany in western France, where they are still spoken, but by ever-diminishing numbers of people.

Names and Places

The names of thousands of persons are known from ancient documents, and the ancient names of many places have survived to this day. The expansion of Celtic peoples is marked by a spread of place names which preserve the names of the settlers or their language. Galatia in Turkey or Galicia in Spain both mean land of the Celts, or "Galli", as they were known in Latin. Names like Bragança in Portugal, Bregenz in Austria, Brie in France, incorporate the Celtic word "bri" meaning high or great. Bologna in Italy gets its name from its Celtic founders, the Boii people of Bohemia, in the same way as Belgium gets its name from the Belgae and Paris gets its name from the Parisii people. Gods too were commemorated: the river Seine gets its name from the Celtic goddess Sequana; the god Lug survives in the name of the city of Lugo in Spain and, in France, in the city of Lyons, whose name was "Lugdunum" — the "fort of Lug". Celtic words used to describe places often survive: Dublin means "black pool" — "duv linn" — as does the name Lindow, which is made up of the same words, in reverse order. The words "avon" meaning "river", or "pen" meaning "hill", are common in place names in south Britain and Brittany.

❧ Languages ❧

Linguists have been able to use ancient documents to reconstruct now extinct Celtic languages. These are Celtiberian, spoken in north-central Spain; Gaulish, once spoken throughout Celtica; and Lepontic, a form of Gaulish peculiar to the southern Alps around Lake Como.

There were other Celtic languages, but too little has survived for them to be reconstructed. They included Pictish, spoken in northeast Scotland; Galician, spoken in northwest Spain and north Portugal; and probably Lusitanian, spoken in central Portugal and west-central Spain.

The living Celtic languages are Gaelic, spoken in Ireland, western Scotland and the Isle of Man, and the British languages, Welsh, Cornish, and Breton which replaced Gaulish and Latin in western France after the fall of the Roman Empire.

◀ *In the early Celtic mines at Hallstatt and the nearby Dürrnberg mines, the salt has preserved organic materials which usually decay — the body of a miner, killed in a prehistoric landslide, was found at Hallstatt in the 18th century. Many objects made of wood or leather have been discovered, such as these miners' rucksacks. These tell us that the Celts worked hard using efficient methods to obtain resources from their environment.*

Sustainable Lifestyles

The different Celtic groups had very different lifestyles depending on the possibilities of their region. All along the coasts of the Atlantic they were sailors, traders and fishermen. Inland they were efficient farmers and miners. Although they had no cities, they had manufacturing industries which operated at both local and regional levels. These lifestyles persisted well into the modern period, for Celtic peoples were living in balance with their environment. They had worked out appropriate agricultural methods and were well informed about the resources in each of their areas. Their information had probably been gathered over several hundred years, for there is increasing evidence that the historical Celts had been long settled in the areas we still associate with them.

Salt — Preserver of Health

From about 1000 BC the Celts had learnt to extract and process the rock salt of central Austria, in the area around Salzburg, which is still a major producer of this essential substance. Along the Atlantic they had worked out ways of evaporating salt from seawater.

With salt the Celts could preserve both fish and meat, which ensured a year round supply of protein, hence a healthier population. The whole of Celtica is well suited to dairy cattle and salt could be used to preserve butter and cheese — French cheese was just as renowned then as it is now.

The Celts were invariably described by ancient writers as strong and healthy and studies of skeletons excavated by archeologists confirm that the population had a high-protein diet.

▶ *The saltmines were lit by bunches of wooden tapers carried by the miners or stuck into the walls. Many have been found by today's mineworkers.*

13

⚜ *Gold & Silver — Master Miners* ⚜

A healthy population can work harder and there is no doubt that the Celts worked very hard. Mining with hand tools is a demanding task and they mined on a prodigious scale, extracting tin in Cornwall and Brittany; gold, silver, copper and tin in Spain; copper throughout the Alps; and iron, copper and tin in central Europe. The Celts had also located pockets of rarer substances such as the jet-like sapropelite in Bohemia.

⚜ *Wool & Weaving* ⚜

In the upland areas of central Spain, fine-woolled sheep were bred and hand weaving was carried out on a commercial basis within each household. The Celtiberian "sagum" or cloak was famous throughout the ancient world.

▼ *Woollen cloth reconstructed from fragments preserved in the saltmines at Hallstatt. The weave is the herringbone twill characteristic of the western Celts, in a green and brown plaid.*

▼ *Weaving scene engraved on a ceramic jar from a*
hillfort in Sopron, Hungary. One woman stands at
a vertical loom, the warp stretched by weights.
The shuttle is at the top and two heddles are shown.
Behind her another woman spins.

⪼ *Slavery* ⪻

Slavery was an integral part of Celtic life. Slaves were usually captives of tribal war or local people who had fallen into debt. From building to sewing, slaves did most of the work. Their life was probably no harsher than the average servant's, but they were deprived of the very thing Celts prized above all else — freedom.

⪼ *Memory and Tradition* ⪻

Despite their overall good health and physical fitness the Celts lived only half as long as people today, most of them dying under the age of 40. In family terms this meant that people would rarely live to see their grandchildren grow up. People would marry in their early teens. Many girls died in childbirth and many children in infancy. Young men would be exposed to injuries at work and in war, where untreated wounds would prove fatal.

People with a short life span and who do not use writing have a very restricted memory, both of the history of their own families and of their group. This was overcome in practice by a strong oral tradition with an emphasis on poetry which celebrated the history of individual families. Each Celtic chief had a resident poet, whose job it was to memorise and recite the highlights of that chief's life and that of his ancestors.

⪼ *Hillforts — Celtic Towns* ⪻

There were few cities, though we know of some. Most of these are now covered over by modern towns such as Paris, London and Milan. More common were the hillforts, large hilltop enclosures whose internal arrangements are uncertain, since few of them have been totally excavated. As time went on and the Celts became more like their Mediterranean neighbours, new hillforts, called "oppida" were created. These seem to have been more like modern towns with fairly closely-packed housing and some public buildings. But on the whole, the Celtic lifestyle was a rural one and even the mining areas do not show any great density of population. It seems that in the western areas, each family unit liked to be a little distant from its neighbour.

Farms were usually dispersed, a pattern which persists to this day. In Spain and Portugal, in contrast, there was a preference for more closely packed housing entirely enclosed within the hillforts.

Houses

Houses throughout most of mainland Celtica were rectangular and made of wood, something like the American log cabin and using precisely the same building techniques. There were no fireplaces and a central hearth was used for both heating and cooking, usually in a large iron stewpot or cauldron. Bedding was of straw covered with woollen blankets. In the western parts, houses were more commonly circular but appear to have been similarly furnished. Household containers were mostly of wood, but fine wheel-turned ceramics were also used. Most households had a vertical weaving loom, propped up against one wall, usually close to the entrance to catch the light from the door, there being no windows.

▼ *The Vettones people of central Spain and Portugal put up life-size sculptures of bulls and boars near their hillforts. It is thought the statues are part of cult practices, intended to safeguard the herds. 2nd century BC.*

❦ *Family Life* ❧

In these societies, death affected the structures of family life. Women did not expect to always survive childbirth or to live long with their husbands, and children might never know their parents. The family unit was therefore not composed of children, parents and grandparents, but of extended families made up of only two generations: the parents' age group and the children's age group.

It seems children were brought up, probably with their cousins, by whichever adults were available, or sent to special schools, such as those run by the druids. Whether at home or at druid school, children would learn about each of their parent's families and would learn that they had passed on to the otherworld after a brief passage through this world.

The duty of every child would be to perpetuate the names of their parents by displaying the required virtues of courage, generosity and wit.

❦ *Home is Where the Heart is* ❧

Because children were not likely to have grown up in their own family's residence, young people were in a sense homeless, their sense of "home" relating more to their family or kin than to any particular place. With the Celts this seems to have had two consequences: firstly they felt no great attachment to their home territory and liked to move from place to place. Usually they moved within their own region, but sometimes they left the bounds of Celtica altogether, as when they moved

◀ Open-sided bracelets and earrings in Hallstatt style, from a wealthy woman's tomb at Saint-Colombe, Burgundy. They are made of gold sheet embossed with geometric patterns. Cup-like ornaments have been mounted onto the earrings. 6th century BC.

along the river valleys of the Danube and the Po to take over ill-defended land. Secondly and somewhat paradoxically, they retained a strong sense of group loyalty, defining themselves partly by the homeland they had been quick to abandon when the opportunity offered and partly by retaining both their languages and their traditional institutions of chief, poet and druid.

The poets and druids were of course the custodians of traditional lore and the chief was the living embodiment of the group's identity and history. In following these individuals, the Celts were actually affirming and maintaining their loyalty to their entire group and its ancestry.

Creating a Celtic Image — Development of Celtic Art

The Celts of Celtica evolved a distinctive material culture as a result of contact with their southern neighbours, particularly the Etruscans and Greeks of southern Italy. These two people offered a vast new market for Celtic goods, which were mostly agricultural products and minerals. In exchange for these staples the Italians could offer luxury products manufactured in their many cities, and warm-climate foods such as olive oil and wine. They also introduced the Celts to coinage and to a money economy, replacing the older barter system.

The luxury imports from Italy attracted a great deal of interest in Celtica and they were both imitated and adapted to local taste. Celtica already had many accomplished

▶ *Bronze bracelet in La Tène style, from France. It is decorated with typically Celtic triple spirals cast in relief in a style very different from the repetitiveness of the earlier jewellery. 3rd century BC.*

craftsmen, weavers, potters, metalworkers and jewellers, who had been producing high quality goods for generations. These goods had been meticulously decorated with repetitive patterns, mostly concentric circles or rectangles and swastikas, a style known as Hallstatt, after one of the salt mining sites in Austria.

The craftsmen were now shown exciting new shapes and objects decorated in styles quite alien to their own such as those decorating Greek ceramics. These dramatic scenes, sometimes framed with twining plants, depicted animals, men and women in quite a realistic manner.

⟪ *La Tène* ⟫

The artisans of Celtica had never depicted nature at all; their style had been strictly abstract and geometric. They obviously became fascinated by the new possibilities introduced by the Greeks and Etruscans and developed a whole new art style, which is usually called "La Tène", after an archeological site in Switzerland.

This style of decoration was not adopted by all Celtic groups. It was hardly used in Spain for instance, but was immensely popular in Celtica. Archeologists use this style as one of their methods in charting the movements and settlement areas of Celtic peoples.

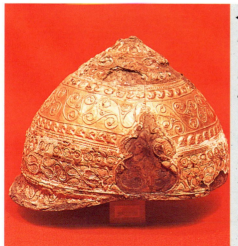

◀ *Helmet from Amfreville, Normandy. Made of bronze, overlaid with iron and with gold sheet decorated with interlocking triple spirals. The lower section is inlaid with red enamel. 4th century BC.*

▶ *Bronze parade shield decorated in late La Tène style with red enamel. Found at Battersea in the river Thames, where it may have been a ritual deposit. 1st century AD.*

≪ *The Torc* ≫

As they came into contact with more foreigners the Celtic peoples seem to have decided to assert their different ethnicity by adopting the use of the "torc" neckring. These are stiff collars which are worn slightly open at the front. They can be made of solid bronze or of hollow tubes of gold filled with wood or iron. They were said to be worn by all the Celts and a great many have been found in the graves of both men and women. They were custom-made, often decorated in La Tène style, embossed onto gold, or cast onto bronze. Some torcs are among the highest achievement of Celtic craftsmanship.

Each region produced its own torc style and it is very likely that different styles served to announce their wearers' ethnic identity or status.

▲ *Twisted gold torcs which belonged to a person of high standing or were votive offerings. Found at Snettisham in Norfolk. 1st century BC.*

▼ *Gold torc from Fenouillet, Haute-Garonne. One of six discovered in 1841, probably from a ritual deposit in water. 3rd century BC.*

▼ *Torc from Mailly-le-Camp, Aube. Made of gold sheet decorated in La Tène style and bent into a tube around a core of wood or leather. 1st century BC.*

⬩ *Trade — Changing with the Times* ⬩

As the La Tène style was being developed in response to influences from the south, other more profound changes were taking place throughout the Celtic world. Trade worked both ways and the import of mass produced objects from the Mediterranean was becoming increasingly significant. Greeks from the island of Phocaea had built a trading port at Marseilles in southern Gaul as early as 600 BC. The Etruscans had built a port at Spina on the Adriatic at about the same time, so that the Celts of the Alps had access to two import-export routes.

Commerce followed politics, and when Greek and Etruscan power dwindled in Italy, as Rome started to develop, the trade went on, though now in Roman hands. This probably improved the ordinary person's daily lifestyle as exotic delicacies such as oil, spices and wine became more easily available.

⬩ *Burials* ⬩

A significant outcome of increased trade was also the rise of personal wealth for some Celtic chiefs. In keeping with the Celtic views on life in the otherworld, these chiefs and their families were given sumptuous burials in tombs. Many tombs have been excavated by archeologists over the past two hundred years. The most elaborate are in the mining areas of Austria and Germany and along the French trade routes, but there are others throughout the Celtic world.

Excavation of habitation sites and religious sites has yielded a lot of information about the Celtic way of life.

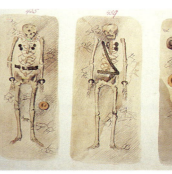

▶ *Detail of illustration of inhumation burials at Halstatt. Over 100 of these burials were excavated in the 1850s and were some of the most important archeological discoveries ever made in Europe.*

Women of Spirit

Celtic women had an unusual degree of freedom by the standards known in the ancient and medieval worlds. They were renowned for their individuality and courage and were particularly praised for their qualities of self-respect and independence. Celtic women could have a high public function, and they could go against the wishes of their families in the choice of a husband.

A high public office for a Celtic woman could be that of priestess, but in Britain two queens are known to have exercised significant political power in the first century AD.

Warrior Queens

Cartimandua

In Yorkshire, Cartimandua, a woman of noble descent, ruled over the people of the Brigantes. She endeared herself to the Romans by handing over to them the rebel chief, Caratacus of the Catuvellauni in 51 AD, after leading a seven-year-long guerilla campaign. She should have protected Caratacus as he had taken refuge with her. Drunk with power, Cartimandua divorced her husband, Vellocatus, and married his armour bearer, Venutius, whom she allowed to rule alongside her. The ensuing civil war had to be fought with Roman help.

Boudicca of the Iceni

While Cartimandua's great power was gained by scandalous means, the other British queen, Boudicca of the Iceni, appears to have acceded to power only on the death of her husband. She may have been entitled to rule in her own right for she had sufficient power to lead not only

▲ *In the ancient world the land was always female, so Gallia, the land of Gaul, was represented by a woman's head. She differs from a Roman woman because of her simple hairstyle which reveals a lack of urban sophistication.*

the Iceni, but all the southern British tribes in rebellion against the Romans.

Boudicca's husband had put his family under the protection of the Romans. On his death the Romans confiscated the royal treasure, Boudicca herself was flogged and her daughters raped. Her campaign lasted several months, destroying among others the Roman towns of London, St Albans and Colchester. Boudicca led her army in the final battle in AD 61. Before the battle began, she and her daughters rode in a chariot before her army reminding each tribe that the British were accustomed to being led into battle by a woman.

She said, as she rode in the chariot wearing "a great gold torc and a multi-coloured tunic folded around her, over which was a thick cloak fastened with a brooch", that, though descended from great ancestors, she was now an ordinary woman charged to avenge the dishonour brought upon her and her daughters. Her last words were to ask that the army respect her not as a queen but as a woman. After her terrible defeat, she killed herself by taking poison.

Women of High Standing — Archeological Evidence

The description of Boudicca's dress would have fitted almost any Celtic woman of high standing. Archeologists have found numerous pieces of women's jewellery, which are among some of the finest products of European craftsmanship. Within Boudicca's own territory of Norfolk no less that 200 torcs (necklaces or armbands made of twisted metal) have been found, most of them made of high quality gold, though none could have been Boudicca's for they are older than her time by at least a century.

◀ *Twisted gold torc from Snettisham, Norfolk, in the territory of the Iceni. The loop terminals would have had a cord passed through them to keep the torc on. 1st century BC.*

In eastern France and southern Germany during the fifth and fourth centuries BC several women were buried alone in magnificent tombs with outstanding art treasures and all the trappings of royalty. There is every reason to suppose these women were rulers in their own right, free to purchase or commission the luxury goods which were necessary to mark their high status in a carefully stratified society.

The woman's tomb at Vix, in Burgundy, contained a four-wheeled cart, fine Greek ceramics, a gold collar of exquisite design with winged horses on poppy-head terminals, and a bronze vessel which could hold more than a thousand litres of wine. This is the largest and finest of all vessels known from the fifth century BC, manufactured by Greek artists in southern Italy and then transported over 1300 kilometres.

Other women's tombs are not quite so richly endowed, but all have fine jewellery, a ceremonial cart and the means to give a great feast, which was in Celtic society the true mark of power.

▶ *Greek bronze crater-vase from the woman's tomb at Vix, Côte d'Or. About 500 BC.*

▼ *Gold neckring, possibly of Italian manufacture, worn by the woman buried at Vix. The ring ends in animal claws and winged horses on a filigree base, which conceal an internal sleeve connecting the ring with the terminals. About 500 BC.*

◀ *Clothing and Jewellery* ▷

While clothing has not survived intact in any of these tombs, there are enough remains of cloth to indicate that Celtic women had a wide range of fabrics, including linen and wool of different weights. The weaves can be quite elaborate with diagonal or diamond twill patterns or tablet-woven braiding.

Complete garments found in the contemporary Germanic "bog burials" of Denmark include a fringed shawl, a long skirt laced at the waist, and a striking full-length woollen dress woven in one tubular piece on a wide loom at which two weavers must have worked side by side.

▶ *Woollen dress from the peat bog of Huldremose, Denmark. The dress is made of one seamless tube, to be worn pinned at the shoulders. 1st century BC.*

▼ *A woman's jewellery set, made of bronze. It includes a belt, a torc, a bracelet and three safety pin brooches, two of which are linked by a chain. From France, 3rd century BC.*

Buttons were unknown and clothes were normally pinned together with large elaborately decorated safety pins made of gold or bronze. Hair was plaited and heavy neckrings worn.

Celtic women seem to have worn a lot of jewellery, hair clasps, clothes fasteners, finger-rings, bracelets, anklets, glass or amber beads, and the ubiquitous torc necklace. Precious stones were not used but the gold or bronze was covered with cast or engraved ornament of intricate spirals and witty transformation of natural forms such as leaf or animal shapes.

Celtic jewellery has an exuberant playfulness which hints at a delight in nature and a joy in the beauty of simple things. The women who wore these individualised trinkets must themselves have been joyous.

▼ *Women wearing long dresses with tight-fitting sleeves, belted at the waist. They are in attendance on a bare-breasted Celtic goddess. Around her are a lion, birds, a boy and a dog. Silvergilt plaque from Gundestrup, Denmark. 1st century BC.*

❧ *Marriage* ❧

There cannot be joy without freedom, particularly in the choice of a husband. Though Celtic society was patriarchal and fathers normally arranged their daughters' marriages, girls were sometimes free to refuse her father's choice.

Even when the girl could choose her husband she continued to live within her family's territory. Much later Irish sources show that a woman always remained part of her own family, with whom she maintained a strong connection, to the point that children might be more commonly known by their mother's name, though they were entitled to use their father's name. This custom translated even into Christian practice, so that St Columba was normally called son of Eithne, after his mother. Even more strikingly, Jesus Christ was often referred to as "son of Mary" rather than "son of God".

Not all women were in a position to pick and choose, since it was normal to marry a man from one's own social group, with an equivalent "honour price", as it was described in the early Irish laws. In this system, which was of considerable antiquity and was probably common to many other Celtic groups, each person was rated on birth and personal wealth. Compensation for injuries or wrongs was proportionate to the honour price, so that a wealthy woman would receive more compensation, but would in turn have to pay more if she were the guilty party.

The mythical Queen Maeve of Connacht explained what made a good husband:

> *I asked as a marriage portion a man without stinginess,*
> *without jealousy, without fear.*

◀ *Motherhood was so important to the Irish that Jesus was often referred to as 'son of Mary' rather than 'son of God'. This is the earliest known representation in the west of Jesus as son of Mary. Mary wears a necklace and a rectangular brooch on her patterned cloak. The image is on folio 7r, at the beginning of the* Book of Kells, *a beautifully illuminated manuscript now held at Trinity College, Dublin. 9th century AD.*

◈ *Divorce* ◈

As the wife did not become a part of her husband's family she could leave it without stress. The Irish laws make it clear that freedom of sexual choice was of considerable importance and rape of any sort was condemned. This extended to kissing a woman against her will or raising her dress. Rape within marriage was considered just as criminal as rape outside marriage and was grounds for divorce.

The laws on divorce were detailed and practical: a woman could divorce her husband if he brought home a mistress, but she could go on living in the family home. If the husband acquired a second wife the first wife took precedence over her in terms of status and property rights.

A woman could divorce her husband if he failed to support her, or failed to treat her with respect, if he was impotent, homosexual, sterile or gossiped about their sex lives. She could even leave him if he was fat, a snorer or just plain repulsive.

The same criteria were applied to men wishing to divorce their wives. It is interesting that it was considered quite likely that a woman might be in a position to support her husband and legal provisions were drawn up accordingly. The laws show that in Ireland women could be lawyers, doctors, poets and even warriors.

◀ *Women were honoured for their status and wealth — a mirror like this one from Desborough would have signalled a woman's high position in the society.*

In cases of divorce, the property was divided up according to "honour-price" and how much each person had contributed in household goods or cattle. Because of these provisions we are reasonably well informed about women's property. Weaving was obviously highly valued, as it was throughout the ancient world. A woman was entitled to a complete set of weaving implements and had copyright over her designs. She also owned her jewellery and household implements.

Mothers normally obtained custody of the children in the case of divorce, with the father contributing to their maintenance.

Children

Both boys and girls were sent away from home at the age of six or so, to be fostered and educated by people with special skill: doctors, lawyers, poets, craftsmen. This system created strong bonds among the fostered children, which sometimes led to marriage alliances.

Both the Irish and the Welsh practised fosterage, but in Wales only boys were sent away, probably to preserve Welsh girls' virginity. In Ireland virginity was not emphasised in marriage contracts until the introduction of Christianity; whereas in Wales, which had been under Roman rule, there was a virginity fine to be paid by the father if a girl proved not to be a virgin at marriage.

In either country the marriage itself was not a religious ceremony, but simply an acknowledgment before witnesses, accompanied by the inevitable feasting.

The Household

We know very little about the actuality of marriage or circumstances of childbirth. The stories, both mythical and historical, indicate that there was a woman's area, possibly a separate building, occupied by the "woman of the house", young children and serving women.

It was clearly the wife's responsibility to run the household and see to it that her husband's guests were entertained in appropriate style.

The feasting hall, the place where private meets public, was the usual setting for dramatic events.

⟨ *Fidelity* ⟩

Over and over again the stories, both mythical and historical, make clear that marriage was a working partnership intended to enhance each spouse's status.

The wife, the husband, the girlfriend and the bishop

The following story is a telling picture of marriage in a society where status and honour are the most important considerations.

> *Once upon a time Bishop Moel came to Dubthach's house and he saw Dubthach's wife in grief; so he asked: "What sorrows you?"*
>
> *"I have great cause for grief," she said, "for more dear to Dubthach than I is the handmaid that is washing your feet."*
>
> *"You have good reason," said Bishop Moel, "for your child shall serve this handmaid's child."*
>
> *The handmaid's child was Brigit, who became a patron saint of Ireland.*

In this story the wife is upset not because her husband is unfaithful but because she has been shamed by his taking a girlfriend from one of her own servants. But the wife is seizing the opportunity of humiliating the girlfriend in front of an important, and saintly, guest, at whose feet the girlfriend is in fact kneeling throughout this unpleasant little scene.

◀ *The Gundestrup cauldron which had been ritually placed in a bog in Denmark. It is covered inside and out with depictions of divine beings and their attendants. This side shows a naked goddess with a headband and a Celtic torc. 1st century BC.*

A Woman's Honour

Honour was everything to Celtic women as well as men. This point is made in this early story of the Galatian Chiomara, which came from the defeat in 189 BC of the Galatians by the Romans.

> *Chiomara, wife of the local chief, was captured in battle and raped by a Roman officer. When a ransom was arranged, she was brought by her captor to the agreed place, a river crossing. A Galatian warrior crossed the river and handed over the gold. As soon as this was done Chiomara gave a signal to the warrior to strike the Roman officer who was passionately embracing her for the last time. The head of the Roman rolled onto the ground. She picked it up, wrapped it in her cloak and fled across the river back to her husband.*
>
> *When Chiomara reached her husband she threw the head down in front of him. Amazed, he said to her: "What a faithful wife you are." "Yes," she said, "but above all I would not let that man live to boast of having had his way with me."*

The story makes it clear that Chiomara is acting on her own, that she has the status to direct a killing in circumstances which are potentially dangerous and that she is less concerned with her husband's views than with her own self-respect. She is not in the least squeamish about picking up a bleeding head and carrying it around with her. She also gets the last line, as she has a good way with words — another trait highly prized throughout the Celtic world.

▶ *The Tara Brooch. A ring with a heavy pin attached to it. Both are plated with gold panels of filigree animals and spirals, spaced out by amber and enamel studs. A safety chain is atttached to the ring. 8th century BC.*

⊰ *Women's Independence Diminishes* ⊱

The independence of Celtic women diminished over the centuries as the Celtic nations were overrun by powerful enemies, but in areas where tradition could be maintained some women managed to retain status and respect.

The most flamboyant is certainly Gráinne Mhaol, the lady pirate who in the 1590s harassed England's Atlantic fleets from her headquarters at Clew Bay on Ireland's west coast. She is often described as a nationalist, but she had no qualms about raiding Irish-owned ships or land.

Though married twice she retained her own family name, as did most Irish women until the modern period.

Gaelic poetry written by women gives us a direct access to the way in which they thought about themselves and their world. In this, one of the greatest of Irish medieval poems, the poet laments her decision to leave her lover in order to become a nun.

Liadain,
That is my name and Curithir
The man I loved; you know my sin.
Alas too fleet!
Too brief my pleasure at his side;
With him the passionate hours were sweet.
Woods woke
About us for a lullaby,
And the blue waves in music spoke.
And now too late
More than for all my sins I grieve
That I turned his love to hate.
Why should I hide
That he is still my heart's desire
More than all the world beside?

Reflections of the Past

The independence and eloquence of Celtic women are not easily wiped out and these qualities are very evident in another peasant poet, Máiri Mhór nan Oran (Mary MacPherson).

Though she was of humble origin and had a prison record, her mastery of traditional Gaelic poetic forms enabled her to speak for an otherwise unheard people. Writing in 1887, she described the brutal crushing of a popular uprising on the isle of Skye in 1882:

> *And the women who were kind and generous*
> *And who were of courteous manners,*
> *Had their skulls shattered*
> *In the braes of Ben Lee*

This passage commemorates the role of women in the "crofters' war" of late nineteenth-century Scotland, a battle for land rights in the Highlands and Islands. Because the men were mostly away, working as fishermen or labourers elsewhere, many of the croft farms were worked by women, who seemed easy prey to rapacious landlords and their hired police.

The Gaelic women, however, put up a vigorous fight and eventually won — at least the moral victory. In speaking for them, Máiri Mhór used a language, images and ideas of honour which would been very familiar to Chiomara, or the Lady of Vix, or Queen Maeve.

▶ *The Roscrea Brooch from Ireland, a heavy silver cloakpin. The head is decorated with gold panels of filigree animals and studs of amber. 9th century AD*

Chiefs and Warriors

The historic Celts were famous warriors and courage was considered to be an essential virtue in both men and women. Fighting was a display of courage, often with no fixed purpose — nobody gained anything but fame from some encounters.

Such actions stem from two feelings held by the Celts: one that life was of little importance, since the real world lay beyond this one; the other that memory is short and the only way to live on in people's minds is to perform outstanding deeds. To be forgotten is the real death; physical death is just the moment of passage to that otherworld where one will be treated according to the glory of one's deeds in this world. The Irish hero Cúchulainn says he is happy to live only a single day on earth if he can live for ever in the memories of men.

◄ *Coin showing a human-headed horse drawing a war chariot which is being attacked by a warrior below. The significance of the half-human horse is unknown. He is probably a horse god or a supernatural being representing the fury of war in general.*

The Warrior Image

The early Celts did not much care to depict the human figure but there are some images of warriors. One is embossed onto the backrest of a bronze burial couch and shows a man waving a curved shield in one hand and a long sword in the other. He is standing on the platform of a four-wheeled cart, which is drawn by two stallions — not by the normal draught animals. The warrior might be naked and he is certainly not protected by his shield, which is held well away from his body. As a warrior cannot fight in this position and is indeed highly vulnerable to a flung spear or arrow, the scene is not of batttle but of challenge. The warrior must be challenging an opponent to single combat and his position is thus one of heroic defiance. This image was made around 500 BC and buried in a tomb at Hochdorf, near modern Stuttgart, in Germany.

From much the same place and time comes another image, this time a lifesize carving of a naked warrior, with an erect penis. He wears only a small pointed hat, a neckring and a large belt. His arms are crossed over his body, the right hand

▶ *Life-size stone statue of a warrior, which originally stood on top of a burial mound at Hirschlanden, Germany. The collar, belt and hat are the same as those found at Hochdorf. 6th century BC.*

grasping the pommel of a dagger which is passed through his belt. As he is obviously aroused, he is probably drawing his dagger for action. The left hand is placed on his right breast in a gesture which is not understood, but suggests a movement before or after speech, part of a challenge or an oath.

The remarkable thing about this statue, which once stood on top of a burial mound, is that archeologists have recovered the body of a man who could have served as its model. He wore the same pointed hat, a gold neckring, and a wide gold wide belt with a gold-sheathed dagger. The only difference is that the statue stood about 1.7 m (5 ft 7 inches) high, while the real man was a veritable giant, 1.9 m (6 ft 3 inches) in height. He was buried in the Hochdorf tomb, lying on a custom-made bronze couch, decorated with the image of the warrior on the cart and with another scene of a pair of men either doing a sword dance or engaging in a real sword fight. In the Celtic mind fighting had a ritual nature and could be expressed as much in a dance as in an actual contest.

▼ *The gold cover and bronze scabbard for a dagger found at the waist of the man buried at the tomb in Hochdorf. He also wore a pair of gold bracelets embossed in Hallstatt style (see page 18).*

▲ *Gold neckring from Hochdorf, similar to the one shown on the stone statue at Hirschlanden (see page 39).*

⋘ *The Buried Chief* ⋙

The Hochdorf tomb consisted of a wooden chamber lined with woollen hangings and enclosed by a rubble filled cavity wall of horizontally laid split logs. The construction of the tomb and of the great earthern mound heaped over it was in itself a major task. It is all the more astonishing, therefore, that this mound was only one of a dozen or so in its area, clustered around the major hillfort at Hohenasperg. The solid construction of the Hochdorf mound had created a sealed atmosphere in which bacterial action was delayed and many organic materials were preserved including textiles and wood.

Like the Lady of Vix the man at Hochdorf was old for his time – she was in her 30s, he in his 40s. And like her he was well-equipped to give a banquet in this or the next life. He had a wine holder of Greek

◀ *Bronze bucket from Halstatt which was part of a banqueting set used to hold mead or wine.*

▶ *Gold plated bowl from a wealthy tomb at Schwarzenbach, Germany. It would have been used to serve wine or mead at a banquet.*

manufacture and a fine stock of drinking horns, some made of genuine ox horn, another made of iron bound with gold. These were displayed on the woollen hangings which lined the tomb walls. A gold bowl sat on the wine holder and was presumably intended as a server. Bronze dishes made up the set and were stored on a four-wheeled cart similar to the one shown on the burial couch.

⟪ *Banquets* ⟫

The banquet was a normal part of the Celtic chiefs' life, for they did not normally inherit chieftainship but were elected to it by their peers. To acquire and retain respect they had to fulfil expectations of wisdom, courage and generosity. In practice, this meant they had to employ poets to sing their praises and entertain on a fairly lavish scale.

The poets accompanied the chief everywhere, even into battle. Their principal function was to record the deeds of the chief and his family and to recite them at banquets.

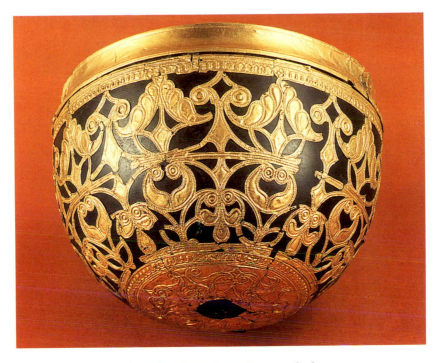

The Chief's Bodyguard

It is noticeable that the Hochdorf man did not have either a long sword or a shield of the sort shown on the burial couch. That sort of equipment was more likely to have been used by the men of his bodyguard, the armed followers who made up the retinue of the Celtic chief and fought on his behalf.

Such men were rewarded mostly by the honour of being the chiefs' champions, but they would also receive gifts of gold or land or cattle, depending on what the chief could afford to give away. There was thus a direct connection between courage and wealth. To be brave could make a man rich; conversely, the wealthier the chief, the better the warriors he could attract. The Greek historian Polybius (?205–?123 BC) described how important it was for Celtic chiefs to have a following, how the chief who had the greatest number of dependents and companions was the most feared and most powerful member of the tribe.

⚜ *War — the Deadly Game* ⚜

Fighting could become a self-perpetuating cycle, in which ultimately the purpose of war was to have sufficient wealth to be able to go to war again. Normally this cycle would stop for lack of funds, there being only enough land, gold or cattle to go around; but it nevertheless created a ceaseless unrest between the various territories.

The large number of hillforts occupied in the years 500 BC and later indicates the uncertain nature of politics in those times. There is also an increasing number of warriors' tombs, in which a man is buried with a two-wheeled war chariot. Such tombs are known right across Celtica and in Britain and are a particularly good illustration of the symbolic nature of Celtic fighting.

▼ *Reconstruction of a warrior's tomb from the Marne, with the body of the warrior laid out on his chariot (the wheel tyre can be seen in the foreground). His spears are at his side and his pointed bronze helmet (shown in the inset) between his feet. Above him lies another body, perhaps his charioteer. 5th century BC.*

◈ *Chariot Fighting* ◈

Chariot fighting requires two men. The driver is normally unarmed. His job is to bring the warrior to battle, where the warrior then takes over, usually in single combat on foot.

This form of fighting requires that the opponent be using the same tactics, in other words that both men observe the same rules. An opponent who does not observe the rules will kill the charioteer, thus disabling the chariot and effectively putting the warrior out of combat. In the Celtic view to kill the charioteer would be dishonourable and in fact an inconceivable act of cowardice.

The existence of such rules of battle underscores the point that Celtic fighting is a contest between two matched opponents, a sort of deadly game, not warfare as it was practised by their contemporaries, the Greeks or Romans.

▼ *Reconstruction of a Parisii warrior's tomb from Garton-on-the-Wold, Yorkshire. In this burial the chariot has been dismantled and wheels placed to one side. The warrior lies in a crouched position with his weapons and jewellery. 1st century BC.*

◀ *Harness fitting of bronze highlighted with yellow and red enamel, which would have flashed and sparkled as the chariot horse ran. The essentially ritual nature of chariot fighting meant the horses and their decoration were important in asserting the status of their owner. From Paillart, Oise, France. 1st century BC.*

⋘ The War Chariot ⋙

The use of the war chariot was made possible by technical developments in Celtica in carpentry and iron production. These developments were interconnected because better tools — made of iron and thus easy to sharpen — enabled the refining of existing woodworking skills. The Celts did not invent the two-wheeled chariot and probably borrowed the idea from their eastern neighbours, but they rapidly learned to make fast lightweight vehicles with a very small turning circle. Some warriors were so surefooted that they could fight on the chariot pole while the chariot was still in motion.

The chariots were relatively low, with the platform about 70 cm (28 inches) above the ground, and were drawn by the Celtic horse which was about 30 cm (1 ft) shorter than the modern horse. The chariots were carefully made, with particular attention paid to the stress points where the platform joins the axle and the axle the pole.

The chariots would have been costly items, which makes it all the more significant that they should be buried with their owners. This suggests that chariots were as much identified with their owners as their swords were.

⟪ *The Warriors' Weapons* ⟫

Swords

The Celts had become particularly skilled in the making of long swords, which were noted for their flexibility — they did not break on impact but bent and could be straightened by the swordsman, even in the midst of battle.

Studies of the hundreds of weapons found either in burials or in shrines have enabled archeologists to trace technical improvements in the design of swords and shields throughout the 4th and 3rd centuries BC. These technical advances show the Celts gave careful thought to the use of their weapons. One problem they had to resolve was the handling of a sword which had originally extended approximately from the hip to the knee, but was now so long as to reach the warrior's calf. They resolved this problem by creating sword chains, fixed to the sword scabbard at one end and to a leather belt at the other around the waist. The weight of the chains kept the scabbard in position, while their curvature and flexibility enabled the swordsman to move unhampered.

◀ *Swords and scabbards of the* La Tène *period, all found in graves in France. The manufacture of swords must have been a major industry, comparable to today's armaments industry. The swords were made of tempered steel and were of impressively high quality — even by modern standards.*

Body shield

At the same time, the Celts developed their characteristic long body shield, which was flat and oval, with a substantial midrib extending down the shield's whole length. The centre midrib was covered with a separate piece of metal bolted on to protect both the shield and its handgrip which was bolted on to its interior. These long swords and shields were used primarily in Celtica, north of the Pyrenees.

◆ *Other Weapons* ◆

South of the Pyrenees, a different sort of weaponry was used; the Celtiberians preferred a shorter sword, not more than 40 cm (16 inches) long, and a round shield. They also used spears and javelins. Hundreds of weapons have been found in the warrior burials of the Spanish Meseta: these are usually single graves containing a funerary urn with the ashes of the cremated body and the warrior's jewellery and weapons. The swords are sometimes bent in two, perhaps to indicate that they too are dead. Other equipment includes spearheads and javelins, sets of daggers

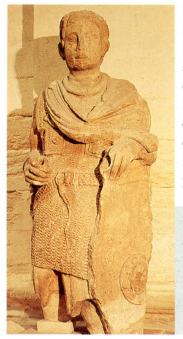

ingeniously fitted into one scabbard, round shields, bronze belt hooks, brooches and neckrings made of bronze, silver or gold. Everything is clearly custom-made and elaborately decorated in distinctively Celtiberian style; the dagger scabbards are particularly elaborate, with silver and copper inlaid into the bronze in interlace and spiral patterns.

◀ *Stone statue of a south Gaulish warrior, from Vachères, Basses-Alpes. He wears a torc, a coat of mail, a chain belt from which his sword hangs on the right, a woollen cloak and holds a long body shield. 1st century BC.*

The Horse

The brooches often show horses and horse riders, for the Celtiberians had mastered the art of fighting on horseback, a development assisted by the fact that they had plenty of land suitable for horse breeding. Celtiberian hillforts were defended against cavalry charges by being surrounded with stones set on edge, something like a modern tank trap.

A mounted warrior is far more impressive than a foot soldier and we have a fine description of such a warrior in Spain from a Roman source.

The historian Appian records that during the siege of Coca, a Celtiberian warrior in splendid armour rode out several times to the Roman lines to challenge the officers to single combat. As none would ever take up his challenge, he would jeer and dance in triumph before returning to his camp.

Warriors for Hire

The Celts of Portugal, like the other Celts, sent their young men away to be trained in age groups. Some of these seem to have become semi-permanent fighting units — gangs who considered the steep mountains their home. The mountains were inaccessible to the Roman army so the Celtic bands, who carried only light weapons, were difficult to capture.

▶ British coin depicting a horseman with a spear and the characteristic body shield. Stirrups were not then used and the spears were thrown during the cavalry charge. Horses were quite small, as can be seen from this image. 1st century BC.

▲ *Duel between Celtiberian warriors, painted on a ceramic jar from Numantia, Soria. Each wears a helmets and short trousers with a broad belt and holds a round shield. One has a javelin, the other a short sword. 2nd century BC.*

▶ *The ideal Celtic chief: bulging eyes, bristling eyebrows, sweeping moustache and stiffened hair all show the warrior's ferocity while the torc shows his heroic status. Carved stone head from Msecké Zebrovice, Bohemia. 3rd century BC.*

We know of similar bands of armed young men from the much later Irish medieval period, where the men of the Fianna lived in woods, rather than mountains. In even later times, such men were the "gallowglasses" who served with Irish and Scottish chiefs against the colonising English armies.

The general impression of Celtic society over time is that there were more warriors than required, and that many formed fighting units which were available for hire. Such a group were the Gaesatae, or mercenary spearmen, who fought with the Boii at the battle of Telamon in 225 BC. The Greek historian Polybius described how the

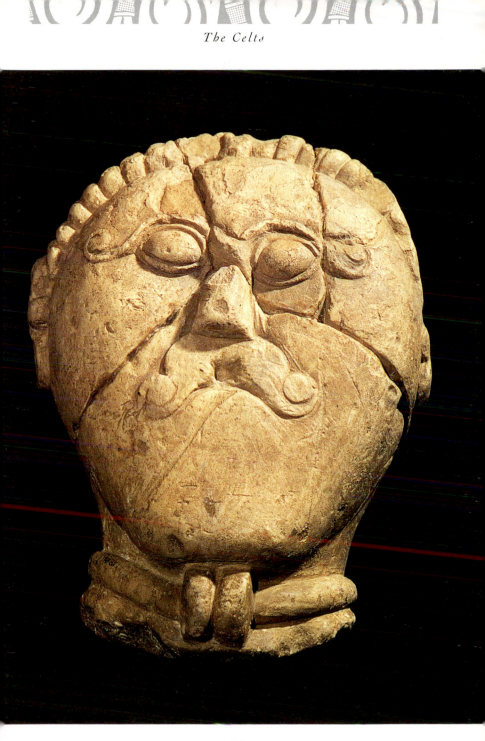

The Celts

mercenaries threw off their clothing in defiance then took up their position in the front ranks naked. Wearing nothing but their arms, their gold necklaces and bracelets, these warriors of splendid physique were a terrifying spectacle.

A chief's normal bodyguard would probably be sufficient only for the occasional skirmish. If a chief decided to go to war he could call on the mercenaries, but he would have to plan well ahead of time, since their services were presumably also available to his opponents. We have descriptions of this process from Britain, in *The Gododdin*, a long poem, attributed to Aneirin, but more likely to be a collection of verses by several poets.

It consists of about 100 stanzas, and commemorates the 300 or so heroes who died in battle against the Anglo-Saxons, some time around AD 600. These men had come from all over Britain to feast for a year at the court of Mynyddog of Edinburgh. Having drunk the chief's mead they were now obliged to fight for him, even though they knew the odds were hopelessly against them. Most died except the poet who sings their elegy. The poet was of course exempt from fighting, since the whole point of fighting is to ensure immortality through his songs:

> *The men who went to Catraeth were famous.*
> *Wine and mead from gold was their liquor,*
> *for a year according to the custom of the tribal leaders,*
> *three men and sixty and three hundred wearing golden torques.*
> *Of all those that hastened from around the over-abundant mead,*
> *but three escaped by the valour of combat:*
> *the two battle hounds of Aeron and Cynon ran back,*
> *and myself spilling my blood in exchange for my inspired poetry.*

▶ *Stone carving of a divine bard from Paule, Côtes d'Armor. He holds a lyre in both hands and wears a torc. Celtic society had poets who composed stories and bards who sang them to music of their own devising. 1st century BC.*

The Word is Law — the Druids

Celtic religion often seems mysterious because its concepts and practices are very different from those of modern, book-based religion. The Celts thought of the visible world in which they lived as part of a much larger invisible world. They viewed themselves as passing through this life on their way to another, possibly to more than one life or shape. The visible world was itself fluid, and both places and things might conceal other realities.

Life After Death

The reality of the otherworld was not in question. The Celts were so certain of it that they would even lend money to be repaid in the next world. They buried or burned letters with the dead, to be read in the otherworld. We have such a letter from Larzac in southern France, written on lead and addressed to the otherworld beings. In it two women ask for help against a coven of nine named witches. People in the otherworld could answer, for instance, by appearing in dreams to those who spent the night near their tombs. When people died, their personal belongings were buried or cremated with them, for use in the otherworld.

True Vision — the Druids

The Celts had a special group of learned men whose function was to act on behalf of the human world in its dealings with the otherworld.

They were called the druids, meaning "people of true vision". They could be men or women who had undergone intensive training in order to understand the workings of both the visible and invisible world. They advised on government and acted as judges in all important cases, both private and public.

In Gaul, cases of national importance were settled at the yearly meeting in the central forest of the Carnutes where people who had disputes to settle assembled from all over the country to accept the rulings and judgements of the druids.

The druids and their associates were so important that they could stop war, even once battle had commenced.

As the Romans described it, not only during peacetime but also in war the Gauls obeyed with great care the druids and bards, both friend and enemy alike. Often when two armies had come together with swords drawn, these men stepped between the battle-lines and stopped the conflict as though they were holding wild animals spellbound.

These peace-making methods were effective only with Celtic believers. The druids' attempt to turn back Roman soldiers from their sanctuary on the island of Anglesey was finally unsuccessful. All along the shore of the island was a dense group of armed warriors with women dressed in black like Furies, howling and waving torches. Alongside them druids lifted up their hands to the heavens, pouring out curses. The Roman soldiers were terrified by this sight. But their paralysis was momentary, and in the end the island was lost.

An Oral Tradition

Druidical knowledge was entirely oral and memorised. There were schools, which could be attended for up to twenty years, much the same length of time as it takes today to go from primary to tertiary education. For specialised training, students would go to Britain where druidism was said to have originated.

At the end of all this training the druids were considered so wise their decisions seem never to have been questioned. They had considerable authority and while the Romans appeared to have banned druidism in an attempt to destroy this far-reaching influence over Celtic society the druids continued to exist as healers and diviners until at least the fourth century AD in Gaul and until the seventh century in Ireland and Scotland.

⋘ *Messages from the Otherworld* ⋙

Beings from the otherworld would communicate by disturbing the natural order of things. In order to understand the meaning of these disturbances, the druids had to be familiar with that natural order, the system of nature which the Greeks called natural philosophy. The Roman consul Cicero was told that predictions were made by interpreting signs and omens and by a process of reasoning based on certain facts or premises. Events happening out of season, such as an unexpected snowstorm, would be significant; so would something abnormal, such as a raven with a white wing or mistletoe growing on an oak tree.

⋘ *Astronomical Calendar* ⋙

The most common form of prophecy in the ancient world was the study of the movement of the heavens, since the stars and planets follow regular patterns which are unlike anything observed on earth. This form of prophecy would be for general use on a day to day basis, but in addition could serve to schedule particular events. For this purpose the druids devised a special calendar. We have two versions of this calendar, both from central Gaul, which were engraved in bronze towards the end of the second century AD.

The calendar is a perpetual one, with five years made up of twelve lunar months, plus two intermediate months, intended to bring the lunar months into line with the solar year of 365¼ days, a complex and original system which must have taken centuries of astronomical observations to devise. Each month is divided into two halves, and each day is marked by a hole punched in the bronze, into which a peg could be inserted as a marker.

▶ *The calendar from Coligny, Ain. A framed bronze sheet, originally mounted onto a wall, later smashed and buried. It names the twelve months of a 355-day year, plus two additional months added to create an accurate five-year cycle. 2nd century AD.*

On the Coligny calendar some days are inscribed "good" or "bad" and there is also a sentence which has been translated "the three nights of Saman". This refers to the Celtic winter feast of the 1st of November, which has survived to this day under the name of Halloween.

Death is the Messenger

To send a message to the otherworld more active methods had to be employed. One was to kill a man by stabbing him in the back or the breast in order to study the way he died. This method may have been based on the idea that the moment of death is the point where this world meets the other. The dying victim passes into the otherworld which then uses his body's death throes as a return message for the druids to read.

In times of stress, when extra help was needed from the otherworld, killing became a focus of religious ceremonies. These sacrifices were

supervised by the druids who were responsible for making sure procedures were carried out correctly.

People suffering from serious illnesses and people involved in the dangers of battle made, or promised to make, human sacrifice — the druids officiated at such sacrifices. They believed the gods preferred it if the people executed had been caught in the act of theft or armed robbery or some other crime; but when the supply of such victims ran out they would go to the extent of sacrificing innocent people.

⟨ *Lindow Man — Archeological Evidence* ⟩

From the archeological evidence it is clear that ritual killing increased when the Celtic world came under stress from the systematic attack by Rome from the second century BC to the first century AD.

The best-known killing is that of the man found in the Lindow peat-bog in western England who had suffered a "triple death". He had been pole-axed, strangled and then had his throat cut. Similar killings are recorded from Germanic Scandinavia at this time.

◀ *Bronze statuette of a Celtic woman dancing, a gift to the goddess of the waters. Found in a healing spring in central France. 1st century BC.*

▶ *Body of the man found immersed in Lindow Moss, Cheshire. The man was found to be in his twenties, with no scars. His hands were well-cared for which has suggested to some that he was a poet or druid — or at least sufficiently wealthy not to have to work with his hands.*

It is interesting to note that both the Lindow Man and the Grauballe Man from Denmark had well-tended hands, and were obviously not manual workers. They were probably of high rank and would have been considered more valuable victims for an important cause. They may even have chosen to die, the better to represent their people.

Shafts have revealed other ritual killings. Some of these shafts are as deep as ten metres (11 yards) and filled with a variety of offerings, including portions of bodies, which probably represent human sacrifices.

⬤ *Victory Trophies* ⬤

As victory in battle was a gift from the otherworld, part of the gains from that battle were given back. This was done by simply leaving some of the wealth in an appropriate place, or depositing it in a lake. As well, the bodies of the enemies were burnt as offerings and many of the prisoners sacrificed.

But the heads of the more significant opponents would be cut off by Celtic warriors and kept as battle trophies. On leaving the battlefield the warriors fastened these heads to the necks of their horses. Once home they nailed them up at the entrances to their houses. Celtic warriors embalmed the heads of distinguished enemies with cedar-oil, and showed them off to strangers. They would not part with their trophies, even for the equivalent weight in gold.

◀ *Silver disc, part of horse harness. It shows a triskele, surrounded by twenty human heads with stiffly-combed hair and moustache. From Cenomani territory at Manerbio, Brescia. 1st century BC.*

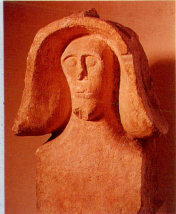

▲ *Stone portico with head-shaped holes to display the skulls either of enemies or of ancestors. Part of a timber and stone sanctuary in the Salluvii hillfort of Roquepertuse, Bouches-du-Rhône, France. 3rd century BC.*

▲ *Stone bust of a warrior, from a shrine near Nîmes, Southern France. The head could represent an ancestor who died in battle, or may be a generalised image showing death-in-life.*

The Human Head — A Source of Great Magic

Images of heads were a common motif in early Celtic art and there seems little doubt that the head was credited with enormous magical powers. Head shrines are known, though only from southern France in the second century BC. Skulls have been found with nail holes through the forehead, and stone lintels have skull-shaped niches cut into them, presumably to display the trophy heads.

Trophy Sites

Two trophy sites of similar date have been found in northern France, though they do not show evidence of a head cult. The one at Ribemont had thousands of human bones, many of which had been used to construct square platforms on top of cremation pits. The much smaller one at Gournay had ditches packed with animal bones and quantities of weapons. Massive quantities of other offerings were placed in pools or lakes throughout western Europe.

▲ *Four stone death masks. Part of a shrine decoration from Entremont, Southern France. 3rd century BC.*

▼ *These two heads may be those of a god of the threshold or boundary, marking the area where the sacred space meets the profane. From Roquepertuse, Southern France. 3rd century BC.*

⋘ *Sacred Places* ⋙

In addition to these places of sacred offering, there were other places used for religious ceremonies and for various assemblies, including the law courts presided over by the druids. These places did not normally have permanent buildings but, as time went on, some were re-used as the sites for Roman temples and later for Christian chapels.

The successive remodelling of these places makes it very difficult for archeologists to get a clear picture of the first activity, but it has been determined that the early Celtic sites were simply large open areas enclosed by a ditch and earthen bank.

As the otherworld and its inhabitants were ever present, there was probably no need for formal places of worship. Neither was there much need for formal worship. It is worth noting that the various references to druids talk about their organising ceremonies; they do not connect them with particular gods.

▲ *Pair of gold torcs and bracelet, found buried with 45 gold coins as a ritual deposit beside a cult pillar. From a fortified town at Niederzier, Rhineland. 1st century BC.*

⚗ *Gods and Beings from the Otherworld* ⚗

No gods are mentioned in the Coligny Calendar, which suggests that the druids did not worship specific gods, but rather imagined all beings from the otherworld as being potentially helpful. Some otherworld beings are named in Roman or Gallo-Roman sources: Maponos the young god, Taranis the thunderer, Cernunnos the horned one, Lugus the god of crafts, Teutates who protects the tribe, Epona the horse-lady, Rosmerta the goddess of wealth, Cathubodua the goddess of war.

◈ *Seeing the Unseen — Images of the Otherworld* ◈

Originally the Celts did not make images of these otherwordly beings. Indeed they thought it was ridiculous to think that the otherworld could be represented and laughed when they saw statues of Greek gods at Delphi, which they attacked in 279 BC. Later, however, as they came under Roman influence they started to represent some of these beings, though often in an allusive or ambiguous manner.

One of the most interesting images is the phallic pillar from Euffigneix, in the Champagne area. The top of the pillar is a human head with a torc. On the front of the body is a wild boar ("torc" in Celtic) and at either side are two enormous eyes. This presumably represents a boar god, but we can only guess what this god might do.

▶ *Limestone pillar with human head from Euffigneix, Haute-Marne. The hair is knotted at the back (not shown) with two longer pieces tucked into the torc. 1st century BC.*

▶ *Antler-headed god holding a ram-headed snake and a torc. He wears a torc, a long-sleeved shirt, a belt, knee breeches and laced shoes. Around him are plants and wild animals. From Gundestrup, Denmark. 1st century BC.*

A clue is given by the fact that the word "torc" in Gaelic means not only boar but also "hero", so that this statue might be of a god of heroes, or of war. He might appear in dreams in the form of a boar.

There are many other mysterious images of this sort, particularly in France, where they may represent a local divinity: a ram-headed snake in the southeast, a triple-headed human in the north, a human-headed horse in the west.

The ordinary person could communicate with these beings on a daily basis; they could ask for their help or advice, by going to places which might act as a channel to the otherworld: tombs, wells dug into the ground, lakes or high places. All of this seems to have been done with reverence but without a great deal of formality.

In Spain and Portugal there are hilltop shrines which consist of rocks with large cavities to hold rainwater or the blood of sacrificed animals.

▼ *Ritual site in a hillfort at Ulaca, Avila. The site is a large rock outcrop, partly cut away to create a rectangular platform from which rises a flight of steps with cavities cut alongside, possibly to allow the blood of animal sacrifices to flow down in a public gift to the gods of the underworld.*

Throughout Gaul and the British Isles there were sacred wells, some of which continue in use to this very day. Normally these wells were considered to have healing properties.

During the Roman period, they often became important spas, such as Vichy or Evian in central France, or Bath in south England. In the Christian period they became associated with the local saint, St Martin in France, St Brigid or St Patrick in Ireland, and chapels or other shrines were often built around them.

In the Celtic period, however, they were not usually enclosed or built upon, and the worship is marked primarily by deposits of offerings, asking for favours, or giving thanks for favours received.

One of the most famous is at Chamalières, outside Clermont-Ferrand, in central France. Around a thermal spring was a patch of marshy ground literally packed with over 5000 wooden carvings which seem to have been planted upright around the healing spring, during the first half of the first century AD. The carvings depict parts of the human body, limbs, heads, stomachs. There is a beautifully expressive life-sized head of a woman with a torc, but most of the carvings are not realistic. There was no formal shrine. Among the carvings a small lead plaque was found with an inscription in Gaulish which was difficult to read, but was apparently a message to Maponos, the god of youth, from seven named men who also invoke the god Lugus.

▶ *Carved wooden head. Votive offering, deposited as a prayer or in thanksgiving, near the headwaters of the river Seine. 1st century BC.*

The Right Rite — A Practice of Medicine

As systematic students of nature the druids were well informed about the healing properties of various plants and much of Gaulish knowledge was collected in Roman works on medicine. In these works the druids were occasionally ridiculed because of their elaborate rituals for obtaining the more powerful plants, but it must be understood that from the druids' point of view it was perfectly logical to use special rites. In their scheme of things illness was abnormal and thus a message from the otherworld, so healing could be seen as interfering with this message and with the otherworld.

One way to placate the otherworld was to make offerings at the right time. The druids would take mistletoe from oak only on the sixth day of the moon.

When preparation for a sacrifice and feast beneath the trees had been made, the druids would lead forward two white bulls with horns bound for the first time. A priest in white clothing then climbed the tree and

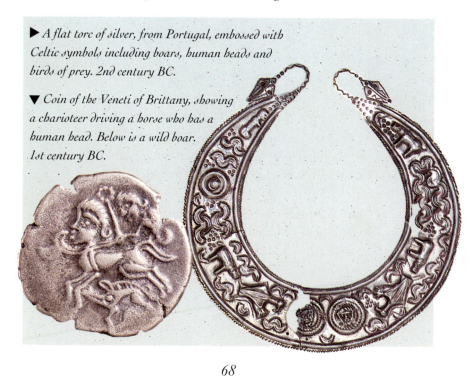

▶ *A flat torc of silver, from Portugal, embossed with Celtic symbols including boars, human heads and birds of prey. 2nd century BC.*

▼ *Coin of the Veneti of Brittany, showing a charioteer driving a horse who has a human head. Below is a wild boar. 1st century BC.*

cut the mistletoe with a golden sickle, catching it in a white cloth. They then sacrificed the bulls. The druids believed that mistletoe, when taken in a drink, would restore fertility to barren animals and was a remedy for all poisons.

As plants are being killed, Nature itself is being offended, so the plant-gathering has to be approached with extreme caution, to protect the druid, and ultimately the patient, who is also placed in danger of disrespect. Both magic and medicine have to be combined in the healing process.

"Selagos", a plant used in fumigation for eye problems, should be cut furtively, without the use of iron, and placed in a white cloth. The druid would be dressed in white with clean bare feet, and have made offerings of bread and wine beforehand. "Samolus", a marsh plant used to cure animal diseases, was to be picked with the left hand, after fasting.

Druids also had faith in fossil sea-urchins, which they thought were made of snake's saliva and which they called the snake egg. These were to be collected only at a particular time of the moon and would bring luck in law cases.

Druids — Guardians of the Celts

The druids were the guardians of Celtic culture. Because they understood the relation between this and the other world they could keep the balance between the two in a world view which was essentially timeless, since past, present and future were in continual interaction. The druids' job was to keep that interaction in harmony.

As the Celtic world was absorbed into a Roman world which made clearer distinctions between this life and the other, the druids lost their purpose. They continued to practice their skills, as doctors, lawyers or even magicians, but the spiritual basis of their authority had gone and their time had passed.

Encountering the Other — The Celt as Wanderer

The desire for wealth was an inevitable outcome of the Celtic thirst for glory. Wealth was required for personal display, for the great banquets the chiefs had to give, and for maintaining military superiority in an increasingly hostile world. In the years after 500 BC a new and seemingly inexhaustible source of wealth presented itself to the people of Celtica, as they came more and more into contact with the wealthier peoples of the Mediterranean.

At first the Celts traded with these peoples in a simple exchange, until they realised that there were not only goods but also land to be had in these southern countries. This information was likely to have come from the Celtic traders who travelled over the Alpine passes into Italy or down the Rhône valley towards Marseilles, but also from the Lepontic Celts already living in the southern Alps and as far south as the river Po in northern Italy.

Across the Alps

The Lepontic Celts played an important part in connecting Italy with Austria. They transmitted the use of writing in the Etruscan script which they themselves had used as early as 600 BC. From Celtica they acquired technical know-how, principally in carpentry and sword

making, and from Italy the use of bronze wine jugs and other banquet implements. They may even have introduced the very idea of the banquet to the Celtic chiefs, for it was a practice well known in Italy, both among the Etruscans and among the Greeks.

The Lepontic Celts may have been the first settlers at Milan and possibly Brescia, but they were soon to be overtaken by their fellow Celts moving in large numbers from the northenmost Alps. These groups started to move some time in the fifth century BC and were well settled by about 350 BC all along the Po valley, a land of heavy alluvial soils for which the agricultural methods developed in Celtica were ideally suited. This area now became known as Gallia Cisalpina, which means "Gaul on this side of the Alps". The Celts stayed in Italy for over 200 years, but continued to have contact with their homelands, to which some eventually returned.

▲ *Celts pillaging a sanctuary, probably Delphi, carved on an Etruscan sarcophagus. The warriors are shown with typically Celtic weapons such as the long body shield. Some of the plundered vases litter the ground.*

⁕ *A Sense of Identity* ⁕

It was living in Italy that caused the Celts to perceive themselves as one people for the first time. Until then they had been separate ethnic groups, though sharing a language and material culture. Now they found themselves to be quite different from their neighbours. The Etruscans belonged to a completely different language family. Both they and the native Italians had a very different material culture to that of the Celts: they lived in cities and had an abundance of mass produced goods, a concept that was unfamiliar to the Celts.

The net effect seems to have been twofold: firstly the Celts started to assert their own ethnicity. Women, for instance, continued to wear the fashions of their original homeland, in a very conservative manner. The warriors continued to use the long Celtic swords but they adopted many other aspects of Italian weaponry, particularly the helmets,

◀ *Iron helmet covered with sheet bronze incrusted with coral and decorated in Celtic style. The rather dull, functional Italian helmet has become a gorgeous object. Such a helmet may have been worn by the Celtic chiefs who stormed into central Italy and sacked Rome in 385 BC. Found in southern Italy, at Canosa di Puglia. 4th century BC.*

▶ *Iron weapons from a warrior's tomb at Batina, Croatia. There are shield fittings, a helmet, a spearhead, a sword and parts of a scabbard decorated in La Tène style. These weapons are found all along the Danube valley and mark the advance of Celtic armies to the east as far as Greece and the Black Sea. Not all of these warriors would have been ethnically Celtic, for there is some evidence of a mingling of the incoming Celts with local Illyrian and Dacian people. 3rd century BC.*

▲ *Gold beads found buried at Szárazd Regöly, Hungary. Many of the beads are decorated with gold filigree; some are in the shape of cartwheels, others have small human heads moulded onto the surface. 2nd century BC.*

adapted and redecorated to suit their own taste. They did not build many hillforts, but adopted urbanised ways — they took over the Etruscan towns of Bologna and Spina, and settled in Turin, Milan, Brescia, Verona, Padua and Parma. Although principally farmers, they continued to be warriors and some served as mercenaries in Mediterranean armies.

They also continued to expand, attacking Arezzo and Chiusi in 386 BC and Rome itself in 385 BC. These attacks were later described in several famous passages, which would have very much gratified the Celtic warriors. Livy tells us that they burst into an instant fury and rushed headlong towards Rome, creating havoc all along their route.

The hordes advanced with terrifying speed, urged on by the horrific noise of their savage curses and war-chants.

The Celts occupied Rome for several months, looting and burning, but making little attempt to settle in the city; they did not even remove its stores of grain, which they destroyed. This of course confirmed the Roman view of Celts as people with little sense of reality.

The Celts finally agreed to leave Rome on payment of one thousand pounds' weight of gold, but from that time on they were always described by the Romans as a fearsome and horrible enemy.

Down the Danube — Archeological Evidence

At this same time, possibly encouraged by what seemed to be a resounding military success in Italy, other groups of Celts were moving from east Austria and Bohemia down the Danube valley with little resistance from the technologically less advanced local populations.

The Celts' movements can be charted from the numerous archeological remains found in Hungary, Serbia, Bulgaria and Romania. Their line of advance can be traced at one remove by archeologists: though the invading group built nothing and left few remains, the second generation which occupied the new land built settlements and created extensive cemeteries in which the dead were buried with traditional grave goods, weapons, objects of adornment in the La Tène style, pig bones and pottery.

▶ *Reconstructed wine pourer with bronze openwork decoration, from a tomb at Brno-Malomerice, Moravia. 3rd century BC.*

▼ *Bronze chariot fittings from a wealthy tomb at Mezek, Bulgaria. This tomb is outside Celtic territory but the objects were made in Celtica. 3rd century BC.*

Clearly these Celts moved as entire family groups, for the women are buried with the same fibulae (metal brooches) and neckrings as we find in their homeland. There was also some intermingling with local populations, causing the emergence of mixed groups, such as the Scordisci, part-Celtic part-native, who founded the town of Belgrade.

Along the Danube the Celts were on the whole an innovative force: they had better technology and introduced coinage, wheel-turning of pottery, and some improvements in ironworking. Their most distinctive structures are the "oppida", the great fortified towns. The immediately remarkable thing is their sheer size, many being larger than medieval towns. The surrounding walls also are of impressively massive construction and reinforce the image of Celts of this period as being warlike and in command of substantial resources of material and manpower.

⟪ *The Celts Meet Alexander the Great* ⟫

The eastern Celts clearly kept in touch with political developments in the Mediterranean for they sought out Alexander the Great, when he made his famous incursion north of the Danube immediately after taking power in 336 BC. Alexander made them feel welcome and gave them refreshments. He supposed the Celts were frightened of him, so he asked them what was their greatest fear. They told him they feared no man and only one thing — that the sky might fall on their heads.

▲ *The Celts fearlessly, but unsuccessfully, attacked the sacred site of Delphi in the winter of 279 BC. This was a terrible insult to Greek pride as well as a sacrilege, for Delphi was the sacred centre of the Greek world.*

This story shows not only that the Celts had retained their own culture, but also that Alexander was familiar with it since he offered them appropriate hospitality. His question about fear was probably prompted by discussions with his teacher, the philosopher Aristotle who had written about the Celts, discussing their views on courage. He had come to the conclusion that the Celts were foolish rather than brave, for they knew no fear and therefore should get no credit for overcoming fear. The Celts may have given swords to Alexander, for a gift of Celtic iron was made to the Treasury of Athens about ten years after this meeting.

Celts as Marauders

Though the image of Alexander became an icon for Celts, who based their own coinage on his, they had few qualms about attacking his successors in Macedonia some fifty years later. In 280 BC, under the leadership of Bolgios, they defeated King Ptolemy Keraunos, killed him and paraded his severed head in the traditional Celtic manner.

A year later another leader, Brennos, assembled an army of 150,000 foot soldiers, 20,000 cavalry, and innumerable camp followers, marched south through Macedonia into Greece proper and then, in an act of real audacity, went on to attack Delphi, Greece's most sacred sanctuary and the stronghold of the Greek city treasures. The Celts reached Delphi in the winter of 279 BC but were convincingly and unexpectedly defeated, probably by being hemmed into a pass during a violent snow storm — which the Greeks later chose to think of as divine intervention. Brennos, wounded in battle, killed himself, either at Delphi immediately after the battle, or during his army's retreat to the north.

Some of Brennos' followers returned to the Danube but others stayed around the shores of the Bosphorus, to which other Celtic groups had come with women and children. The men were fighting as mercenaries for, and against, the local kings.

Establishing Galatia

One king, Nicomedes of Bithynia, shipped Celtic mercenaries across the Bosphorus into modern Turkey. After their defeat by Attalus I of Pergamon, in the 230s BC, they created the town of Ankara and became known as Galatians. They preserved their ethnic identity and customs for a couple of centuries, as shown by this story of typically Celtic extravagance.

Ariamnes, a wealthy Galatian, said he would feast his people for a year. He built large sheds at regular intervals and equipped them with cauldrons. He paid the villages to provide enough wine and grain for a whole year and each day he would send out cattle, pigs and sheep to be slaughtered.

The Celts in Italy

Meanwhile in Italy the Cisalpine Celts were under renewed attack from an ever more powerful Rome, which had already taken over their settlements on the Adriatic in 284 BC. Sixty years later the Boii of Bologna assembled a great army, which included Gaesatae mercenaries, and marched upon Rome, only to be defeated at the battle of Telamon in 225 BC. The Romans then captured Milan in 222 BC, and would

▶ *An idealised representation of Celtic courage: a warrior defeated in battle kills his wife and himself rather than be enslaved by his victor. From the Greek temple at Pergamon, Turkey. The temple was created to celebrate the victories of Attalus I and his descendants over the Celts — or Galatians as they were called in Greek. 3rd century BC. Stories about these strange people were preserved by Greek authors.*

probably have gone on at that time to take Bologna from the Boii, had not Hannibal and his Carthaginians crossed the Alps in 218 BC.

Throughout his overland march from east Spain, Hannibal had received Celtic support, particularly in southern Gaul and in the western Alps. The north Italian Celts must have seen in him the champion who would save them from the increasingly dangerous Romans, but they were to be disappointed for Hannibal left Italy in 203 BC.

The Romans resumed their attacks upon the Boii, finally expelling them from Bologna in 192 BC. Some of the Boii returned to Bohemia, where they built the great fortified settlement of Stradonice and where they will have met some of their kinsmen returning from their adventures in the east.

◁ *The Danube Valley — A Great Expansion* ▷

The Celtic world now extended all the way along the Danube valley, with offshoots right through the lands bordering on Greece and Italy. This world had reached its greatest extent by 200 BC, embracing much

of Austria, Hungary, Serbia, Bosnia, Slovenia, parts of Bulgaria and Romania and extending into Asia Minor. As Celtic groups still controlled the Italian Alps, Gaul, the British Isles, north Spain and Portugal, there was an enormous expanse of territory in which the Celtic language was spoken and Celtic culture was the norm.

◈ *The Symbolic Torc* ◈

There were many shared elements among the various groups, some of which found expression in art. The most striking link between west and east is the Gundestrup cauldron, a set of curved silver-gilt plaques found in a peat bog in Denmark, which have now been reassembled onto a vessel of cauldron shape. They are not of western manufacture and show highly stylised scenes, some of which are of Celtic motifs, and include figures of divinities with a torc around the neck.

The silver-gilt technique is unknown elsewhere in western Europe. Many of the animal figures are clearly of Mediterranean inspiration and the figures are designed in a relief technique best known from Romania and the Black Sea. Such an object might well have been commissioned

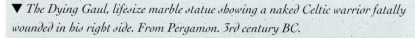

▼ *The Dying Gaul, lifesize marble statue showing a naked Celtic warrior fatally wounded in his right side. From Pergamon. 3rd century BC.*

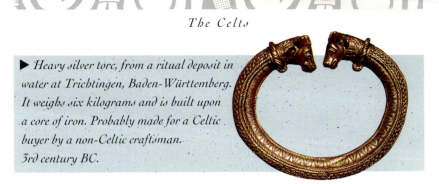

▶ *Heavy silver torc, from a ritual deposit in water at Trichtingen, Baden-Württemberg. It weighs six kilograms and is built upon a core of iron. Probably made for a Celtic buyer by a non-Celtic craftsman. 3rd century BC.*

from a non-Celtic craftsman by an eastern Celtic chief and then sent to the west as part of gift exchange or trade.

A similarly exotic object is the large silver torc from Trichtingen, found in Germany but obviously not manufactured there. Too heavy to be worn, it must be again a gift or offering designed for a Celtic audience, since it is not only a torc but is also decorated with torcs, around the calf heads on the terminals.

The Celtic torc is the major feature on the most famous images of a Celtic warrior, the so-called Dying Gaul. This is an antique marble copy of one of a whole series of bronze statues which were erected as victory trophies in the sanctuary at Athens by Attalus I and Eumenes II, kings of Pergamon who had fought the Galatians. The Dying Gaul is a conventionally heroic figure, shown naked but for a twisted torc, and surrounded by his weapons, oval shield, long sword and long curved battle trumpet. These objects would have been gathered from the battlefield and stored probably in the king's treasury. They are shown also on a carved altarpiece from Pergamon itself and on the triumphal arch at Orange, in France, revealing once more the essential unity of Celtic craftsmanship across Europe.

▶ *The Gundestrup Cauldron — the scene on the interior shows a procession of horsemen riding away from a giant man with a cauldron. Below them are foot soldiers walking towards the giant. 3rd century BC.*

From Anarchy to Submission — the Hammer of Rome

Romans and Celts had grown up together but they did not grow up equally. The Celts conquered precisely as much territory as the Romans did, but did not hold it: they never created an empire. They came into contact with the same people, in Italy, in Spain, in Greece, but the Celts did not change their own lifestyle whereas Roman life became imbued with Greek thought, technology and art.

"The Celtic Fury"

The difference may well have arisen because in the first two hundred years of their history the Celts were undefeated and seemingly invincible: they had swept south and east in a vast swathe, meeting almost no resistance. The Romans on the other hand had started off, at approximately the same time, as the subjects of an Etruscan power which they had to overthrow. They had suffered several defeats, not least of which was the dreadful humiliation when the Gauls overran their city in 385 BC. The entire city had to be rebuilt; thus the catastrophe was permanently graven into Roman memory.

◀Remains of the Celtiberian city of Numantia, destroyed by Scipio in 134 BC. A Roman town was later built on the same site, a low hill at the junction of two rivers, but it was of little importance as Numantia was now part of a colony and no longer an independent state.

As time went on and Rome became involved in a Mediterranean war with Carthage which ruled north Africa and southern Spain, the memory of "the Celtic fury" dimmed. It revived in its full horror in 218 BC when Hannibal of Carthage stormed into Italy from the north at the head of a mixed Carthaginian-Celtic army. He and his elephants had walked from Spain across southern France and over the Alps.

The Romans now felt they had to crush the Celts once and for all. This was done so effectively that within a hundred and fifty years they had permanently subdued all the Celts of Spain, Gaul and Italy.

A Ruthless Conquest

The first Celtic groups to be attacked were those in Spain and Portugal. The Celtiberians and others put up a stiff resistance to the Romans who waged a peculiarly bloody and treacherous campaign. This conquest was relatively slow, partly because of the rugged terrain of Spain, partly because of Roman inexperience and partly because of the determination of the Celtic groups. Sadly, this determination was consistently hampered by internal conflict between the various local groups.

The Romans attacked Spain in a piecemeal manner, city by city. In 143 BC they attacked the city of Numantia, north east of Madrid. It held out until 134 BC when Rome sent in Scipio Africanus (who later destroyed Carthage). He raised what was virtually a private army of 60 000 men and laid siege to the city, which was defended by only 8 000 men. Scipio displayed a ruthlessness which shocks even today — he prevented Numantia's neighbours from coming to her rescue by cutting off the hands of 400 young men who had planned to ride to the city's help. The Numantines offered terms which were refused and in the end were starved into surrender. But "such was the love of liberty and of valour which existed in this small barbarian town" that many of the Numantines killed themselves rather than surrender.

The Celts and the Romans — A Question of Honour

Scipio's siege of Numantia illustrates attitudes which are visible again and again in the story of the Roman subjugation of Celtic peoples. The Celtic groups never understood the disparity between the two

forces and that the Romans were prepared to behave ruthlessly to achieve success. No Celtic chief would have been allowed by his followers to behave as dishonourably as some of the Roman generals did. Their cruelty and corruption ensured that the remaining free Celts, mostly in Galicia and Lusitania, fought even more desperately. Thus northwestern Spain was not conquered until the year 19 BC.

❧ *Caesar and the Gauls* ❧

The conquest of Gaul was undertaken in stages because the Romans were still protecting themselves from attacks from the Mediterranean. Having secured eastern Spain they overran southern France in the 130s BC. It became "The Province" (modern Provence) and was a very profitable acquisition, rich in foodstuffs and with a large population which could supply fighting men and pay taxes. Its governors were notoriously corrupt and were said to have made fortunes from plundering the shrines where the Gauls deposited the spoils of war in thanksgiving to the gods.

▼ *Triumphal arch at Orange. The archway stood at the entrance to the town and was part of the systematic creation of towns and transport systems in Gaul. Its carvings celebrate a number of Roman victories, including the conquest of southern Gaul. 1st century BC.*

The conquest of inland Gaul was very different from earlier campaigns. It was waged from 58 to 50 BC by only one general, Julius Caesar. Caesar followed a very determined plan, whereas previous Roman generals had been content to attack whomever seemed vulnerable. Caesar also had Gaulish allies who had sought his help against their neighbours. In a pattern which was repeated throughout his campaign, he helped his allies and defeated their enemies, but only on condition that they acknowledge the supremacy of Rome. This simple method was astonishingly successful. Dazzled by the immediate gains, the Gaulish chiefs agreed to most of Caesar's terms. Those that didn't, he soon made comply. By the time the Gauls had grasped the magnitude of Caesar's ambitions the conquest was almost over.

Only one Gaulish chief understood Caesar's vision: Vercingetorix of the Arverni tried desperately to unite the Gauls against the common enemy. But his defeat was inevitable. After centuries of tribal independence the Gauls could not make common cause, and Caesar already held too much territory to be easily shaken. The story of Vercingetorix's stand against Caesar is one of remarkable courage.

Resistance crumbled after Vercingetorix's defeat at Alesia in 52 BC. Caesar managed to win the hearts and minds of several influential Gauls. He was a brilliant orator and a great soldier but he was also a physically impressive man: tall, hardy and very courageous. To the Celts he must have seemed in many ways the perfect chief. His conquest of Gaul

◀ *Bronze statue of a warrior or god from a Gallo-Roman temple at St Maur, Oise. The arms are moveable. He wears body armour over a short tunic, a collar and a buckled belt. He has a bodyshield but no weapons. 1st century AD.*

▶ *Gold coin of Vercingetorix. The head is a standard depiction of a ruler, not intended to be a portrait. 1st century BC.*

opened a vast new territory for Rome, which was now bounded by the Rhine instead of by the Alps. Caesar also invaded Britain, though this was unsuccessful. He did however open the way for the conquest of Britain in AD 43.

By the time Caesar returned to Rome in 50 BC, Gaul was effectively pacified and ready to unite under Roman rule.

Divide and Conquer — Living the Roman Way

After the conquest of Gaul a population of around 15 million Gauls was ruled by only a few thousand Romans, who did not even feel the need for army bases. The upper class of Gaul was offered access to a wider world through education in Latin and the possibility of a political career, either locally or in Rome itself. Local groups were given some measure of self-government, although this was proportionate to their friendliness to Rome. Those who had collaborated with the invaders received political privileges and some exemption from taxes. Those who had resisted could not become Roman citizens and paid more taxes, though this discrimination was later cancelled.

In most of their Celtic colonies, in northern Italy, Spain, Britain and southern Gaul, the Romans divided up the conquered land into 50-hectare lots, most of which was granted or sold to Roman citizens, particularly army veterans. They built new towns and introduced new technology which was, on the whole, beneficial to the Gauls.

Throughout the Celtic world we find that once the conquest was achieved the local people tended to adjust to it, although there were in every case sporadic outbreaks of rebellion for the fifty years or so after the initial takeover. The reason is probably that peace and prosperity were in fact established, and the average civilian was somewhat better off under the Romans than under the former chief.

If the Celtic chiefs were reasonably well disposed towards Rome, as many obviously were, their loyalty was assured by gifts of luxury goods

◀ *Remains of the Roman public baths on the left bank of the Seine, in the city of Lutetia Parisiorum, now called Paris. The baths were later incorporated into a medieval building, which is now the Musée de Cluny. 1st century BC.*

and some access to government. To dispose of less friendly chiefs and their warriors, the Romans devised a really ingenious system. Newly conquered peoples were compelled to send their young men into the army. They would normally be posted far from home and were induced to settle in this new place permanently by being granted land after their time of service. From the Roman point of view this had the dual

▼ *Gravegoods from a wealthy Belgae tomb at Welwyn Garden City, Hertfordshire. It contained Roman amphorae, local and Gaulish ceramics, a silver cup and 24 gaming pieces of multicoloured glass paste. This shows how strong Roman influence was even before the conquest. 1st century BC.*

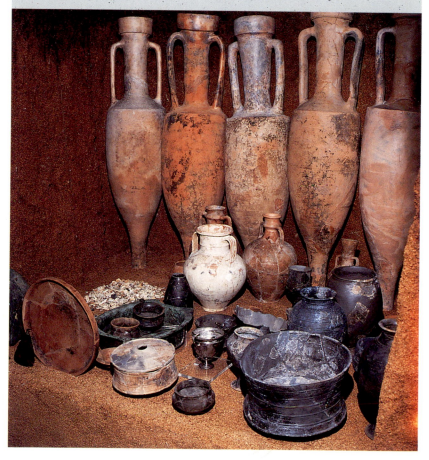

effect of breaking up potentially dangerous groups and creating a uniform Latin-based culture throughout the Empire.

But from the Celtic point of view this system was a disaster. With all the young men gone, Celtic girls had little choice but to marry foreign settlers with whom they could only speak in Latin. As a result, the Celtic languages died out on the continent within a couple of centuries.

Gallo-Roman Religion

In Gaul the death of the language was accelerated by the abolition of the druids, whose teachings had been entirely oral. As they vanished, so too did their knowledge of traditional religion which now survives only in fragments, gleaned from gravestones and dedications to gods. But, as local religious customs were not prohibited if they did not threaten law and order, most of our meagre information about Celtic religion is derived from the Roman Imperial period.

Roman religion was highly regulated, with special priests for different gods and special temples for each one. The Celts had quite different practices, with no priests. Their gods were not worshipped in buildings but in a variety of sacred places: lakes, wells and woods. Sometimes they coupled their gods to existing Roman gods, probably because it would keep the Romans happy and their own gods would get a nice new

Bronze statue of a Gaulish god with the ears of a deer. He sits cross-legged as Cernunnos usually does. From northern France. 1st century AD.

shrine built for them at Roman expense. The new shrine was often in an old cult centre, or close by, and it seems that this was a way of keeping the place sacred. For instance, at Trier, on the Mosel, the Treveri joined their local god Lenus to the Roman god Mars in an elaborate temple of Mars Lenus. This also served for the worship of a goddess, Ancamna, and of the unnamed spirits of two local sub-tribal groups. Celtic divinities were frequently unnamed, or named only vaguely as are the ubiquitous Three Mothers who were obviously the most widely worshipped deities.

Images show how the gods were perceived by their Gaulish worshippers. There is a bewildering variety of representations of both gods and goddesses: some have horned heads, others are shown with snakes, or boars, wheels, hammers, boats, dogs, bears, snakes, birds or the horn of plenty. Roman gods such as Mars, Hercules or Apollo may be named, or identified by standard attributes — Mars' helmet, Hercules' lion skin — but they are also accompanied by other symbols

▼ *A woman with a child at her side, sits with a man (now headless), each wearing a torc. They are surrounded with symbols of fertility and wealth: a bag of coins, a torc, a horn of abundance. On the back of the stone block are carved three smaller gods, including Cernunnos, sitting cross-legged in the centre. From Saintes, Charentes-Maritimes, western France. 1st century AD.*

which are alien to Roman mythology. One of the most famous is probably the ram-headed serpent, which appears on the Gundestrup cauldron, and also on several representations of Mars in Gaul. This is a very old symbol for it was shown already in the fourth century BC, but its meaning is unknown.

From Gaul to France

Celticity was thus alive in popular belief even as Gaul seemed increasingly to become thoroughly Romanised. The old druidical tradition of oral learning and poetical declamation turned out to be very useful for would-be lawyers, and many Gauls became respected members of the Roman bar and administration. Lifestyle became very Romanised: new houses built of stone with underfloor central heating systems and interior decoration of frescoed walls and mosaic floors replaced the traditional wooden buildings. Roman clothing styles were widely adopted by both rich and poor, though usually somewhat modified for the climate — Gaul went on manufacturing and exporting heavy woollen cloaks. Provence (southern France) now acquired the

▶ *Bronze statue of a god wearing a torc, from Bouray, Essonne.*
The torso is human, but the crossed legs end in deer-hooves.
1st century BC or 1st century AD.

▲ *A carving of Cernunnos from the Pillar of the Paris Boatmen, a column showing the principal Gaulish gods erected by the River Seine, where Notre-Dame Cathedral now stands. The stone is very worn, but it can be seen that Cernunnos has torcs hanging off each of his stag antlers. 1st century AD.*

reputation it still has for good food. French seafood, cheese and wine were much appreciated by Roman gourmets, and southern Gaul, at least, became perceived as being a pleasant and civilised place for Romans to live.

Gaul in fact became another Rome. As the empire decayed and finally crumbled, Gaul emerged as the champion of Roman values. There was a brief Gallic Empire in the third century AD which united the old Celtic realms for one last time. It contained Spain and Britain as well as Gaul itself. Its capital was at Trier, an important trading and banking centre and former home of the Treveri. Though the Gallic Empire lasted only from AD 263 to AD 274, the principle of having the capital of the Roman Empire of the West in Gaul had been established. In the fourth century, towards the very end of the imperial period, the seat of government was still at Trier.

≪ *From Roman to Christian* ≫

By a peculiarly Celtic paradox, Roman culture survived in the west through Christianity, which had become the official Roman religion after AD 313. The Gauls adopted and developed the principles of ascetic monasticism, brought to them by St Martin of Tours, who visited the court at Trier towards the end of the fourth century. Monasteries were founded throughout Gaul and they in turn influenced Britain through Martin's disciple, Germanus, Bishop of Auxerre who visited Britain in 429 and sponsored St Patrick's mission to Ireland in the 430s. When Gaul and south Britain were overrun by non-Christian Germanic peoples, Gallo-Roman Christian culture survived in the Celtic lands on the western fringe of Europe — the land beyond the Great Wall built by the emperor Hadrian in Britain.

▼ *Hadrian's Wall was built in the 2nd century AD across northern England as a defense against the Caledonians and Picts of Scotland. It was garrisoned with foreign troops and manned for over two centuries.*

Beyond Rome —
Freedom in the
Celtic Fringe

I n the north of Britain lay the land of the Picts and Caledonians stretching to the fabled Orcades and to the magical frozen sea. The early history of the Picts is unknown but the Irish claimed that some of them had once lived in Ulster, where they were known as Cruithne, the Gaelic form of Briton. The archeology indicates they had been long established in northeast Scotland and in the Orkneys. What little we know of the Pictish language suggests that it is related to Gaulish, but differs significantly from British, which is also a form of Gaulish and is the ancestor of both Welsh and Cornish.

◀ Terminal of a gold torc from Netherurd, Peebles. The style of decoration is that of the Snettisham torcs (see page 22) and indicates contact between the various British groups prior to the Roman conquest. 1st century BC.

◈ *The Painted People* ◈

The Picts had obviously had vigorous contact with their southern British neighbours, from whom they obtained jewellery either as gifts, or as plunder, for they were renowned seafarers and pirates. There were close connections between Britain and the European mainland. The people of southeast England shared a culture and art style with their cousins, the Belgae. The people of Cornwall and southwest England had extensive trading links with modern Brittany, confirming Caesar's mention of Veneti fleets able to undertake the difficult journey from Brittany across the English Channel.

Roman goods had been traded for over a century and the Romans were well-acquainted with the desirable resources of Britain, valuable minerals such as tin in Cornwall, gold in Wales, lead in the Pennines. By the end of the first century AD these areas had been conquered and the marauding Picts sealed off by two great earth and stone ramparts: the Antonine Wall between modern Glasgow and Edinburgh, and Hadrian's Wall which runs just south of the modern Scottish border from the Solway to the Tyne.

Caesar described southern Britain in 54 BC and much of what he says has been verified archeologically: for instance the use of war chariots and hillforts. So it may be reasonable to accept his unverifiable statement that the people of inland Britain painted themselves blue,

▶ *Bronze bracelet with red and yellow enamel decoration from Pitkelloney, Perthshire, weighing over half a kilogram. The style, massive and colourful, is distinctive of eastern Scotland and may be associated with the ancestors of the historical Picts. 1st century AD*

▲ *Bronze trumpet-mouth in the shape of a boar's head from Deskford, Banff.*
When found in 1874, it contained a wooden tongue on springs, which would have
vibrated when the trumpet was blown. 1st century BC.

especially since the discovery of tattoo marks on the Ice Man indicates that tattooing was known in Europe for two thousand years prior to the development of Celtic culture. If we accept this we can accept that the name Pict is not a Celtic name, but a Latin nickname meaning "painted".

A Druidical Site

Another important point made by Caesar was that druidism had been invented in Britain and that young Gauls went to study there. This seems quite plausible given that Britain is known to have had a long tradition of astronomical observations, evidenced in the pre-Celtic sites at Stonehenge and other astronomically oriented stone circles.

The centre of British druidism is said by Tacitus to have been off the north coast of Wales on the island of Anglesey. It is thus of considerable interest that Britain's largest ritual site is in Anglesey at

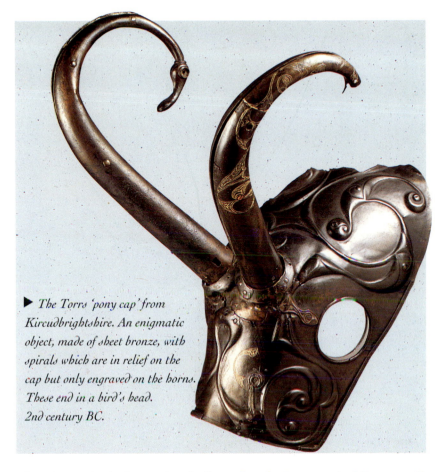

▶ *The Torrs 'pony cap' from Kircudbrightshire. An enigmatic object, made of sheet bronze, with spirals which are in relief on the cap but only engraved on the horns. These end in a bird's head. 2nd century BC.*

Llyn Cerrig Bach. It consisted of a rocky platform overlooking a small lake into which over 150 objects were thrown at about the time of the Roman conquest.

Some of these objects were military equipment of high quality: eleven steel-edged swords; four lance heads, one of which was too long to be useful as a weapon and may have had a ritual use; a decorated shield; an Irish war trumpet; several bridle bits and parts of a war chariot. The most dramatic and unusual find, however, was of two convict neck chains, one with five collars, one with four. As no human bones were found, these are not the chains of sacrificial victims. They are far more likely to be the chains of liberated war prisoners, offered to the gods as thanksgiving.

Non-military material at Llyn Cerrig Bach included animal bones, some ironworkers' tools and fragments of a cauldron. Cauldrons, which are large bronze containers something like stew pots, had both domestic and ritual functions and are found throughout the Celtic world in a variety of contexts. They were used for banquets but they also represented the unifying force of kingship, for the king, said the Old Irish texts, "is a cauldron that cooks every raw thing".

▼ *Bronze scabbard from Lisnacrogher, Northern Ireland — the flowing decoration is lightly incised and cross-hatched. 1st century BC.*

▼ *Detail of a bronze shield mount from Tal-y-Llyn, Wales. It is decorated with the Celtic triple-curved motif. 3rd century BC.*

The Sacred Island

To the west of Britain lay Ivernia or Eire, known to the Greeks as the sacred island. Its people spoke Gaelic, another sort of Celtic language distinct from both Gaulish and British. They seemed mysterious and magical in their cloudy land, which the Romans could glimpse from their garrisons in Wales. The Romans made no attempt to contact the inhabitants of Eire.

The life of the Irish Celts was clearly very different from that of the British. The Irish Celts were far less outgoing, indeed they were almost self-absorbed. Their only contact was with their neighbours in the northeast across a Celtic sea between Ulster and western Scotland.

▶ *Gold tubular torc from Broighter, co. Derry. While the shape is well known among the Belgae of England and Gaul, the decoration appears to be a local elaboration of late La Tène style. 1st century BC.*

▼ *Gold objects found at Broighter, co Derry, in a water deposit. They include the tubular torc, two twisted torcs, two Roman necklaces of fine plaited wire, a bowl, and a unique model boat with a steering oar, seating for eighteen oarsmen and a mast. 1st century BC.*

◀ *Bronze disc from Ireland beautifully cast and hatched to bring out the La Tène decoration. Its purpose is unknown — it may be a lamp. The care expended in designing and making this mysterious object (and several others found which are like it) hints at a society which could afford to educate and support highly-specialized craftsmen.*

From their neighbours the Irish Celts had learnt to smelt iron, to make chariots and horse harness, and to grind grain with a rotary beehive quern (stone hand mill). They had borrowed some elements of British La Tène decoration and adapted them to create their own style.

What they did not borrow is also of interest — they did not use helmets or the long body shield, and showed little interest in representing human beings either on coins or in carvings. Above all they never borrowed the Latin writing scripts which were known to the British. Instead they developed their own writing system called "ogam" which they said had been taught them by the god Ogmios.

Unlike most other Celts, the Irish were obsessed by the past. Their ritual sites are clearly designed around much older sites, such as tombs, about which a rich mythology was developed. The Irish were quite clear that these were not the tombs of their ancestors, but said that they were the homes of an earlier, semi-divine people who had been driven underground by the Celts to the otherworld, where they still resided in the kingdom of the "síd", or fairy-folk. The Irish were equally clear that they themselves were relatively recent newcomers to the island; in medieval times they were to create elaborate legends of their arrival.

◈ *Ritual Places* ◈

Archeologists have found that some ritual places were in more or less continual use for over a millennium. They consist largely of enclosures which surround hilltops but are not fortifications. They sometimes extend over a couple of kilometres and indicate a complex history of use and reuse. The most famous site is that of Emain Macha, in County Armagh, which has been excavated over the past twenty years, revealing a rich history. The major site is an unfortified hilltop enclosure, which produced some unusual finds, including the skull of Barbary ape, mostly likely brought from Spain. At its base is the small lake of Loughnashade, which was used like Llyn Cerrig Bach for ritual deposits. Many objects were found there last century, but were unfortunately melted down for scrap. All that is left are four bronze war

▼ *Emain Macha, co Armagh, one of the 'Celts' ritual sites. A low hilltop enclosure, 290 metres (317 yards) across, surrounded by an earthen bank, now marked by trees. It contained circular timber structures, built and rebuilt for 800 years. The last building phase was in 94 BC.*

trumpets magnificently decorated in La Tène style; these were probably victory trophies for the beings of the otherworld.

The Emain Macha enclosure contained a unique feature, which is dated very precisely through the counting of tree rings to the year 94 BC. It was a large circular structure, 40 metres (43.73 yards) in diameter, and made up of concentric rings of oak posts. This structure was enclosed within a mound of turf, then burnt to the ground and covered with a cairn of stones. In other words the building had been destroyed and buried. The reason for this can only be guessed at, though it is of interest that there seems to have been a change in local settlement patterns after this event. One could imagine that the site was burnt down by enemies and then ritually buried as a memorial by its original owners.

▼ *Tara, co. Meath, the most famous of the Irish ritual sites. The enclosure is about 300 metres (328 yards) across and incorporates older monuments including a 4000-year old megalithic tomb, the so-called Mound of the Hostages.*

The Celts

❦ *The King as Symbol* ❧

Other ritual places in Ireland have been only partly explored, but they too indicate complex histories. Much of these histories must be connected to rituals which are now lost to us. It is worth noting that the myths and legends are centred on these places, including the mythical capitals of Tara, Cruachan, Dun Ailinne, Emain Macha and Uisnech. They reflect the so-called "heroic age" of Gaelic Ireland, known to us through a vast body of stories, some of which were still being memorised and recited well into the nineteenth century.

In these stories, Ireland is described as being divided into five parts, east, west, north, south and the centre. The greatest king is the one who can unite all five parts under one rule. In practice this was rarely achieved, but survived as a poetic ideal, as the poet Tadhg Og O'Higgin expressed it in 1397 in a poem for the chief of Tyrone:

> *Niall O Néill of the nine fetters*
> *brings peace to the land he unites;*
> *having established the five equal divisions,*
> *he goes forth to inspect the borders of Ireland.*

▶ *Carved stone at Turoe, co Galway; one of five such stones in Ireland. It may have marked a ritual site or the boundary of one of the five mythical divisions. The La Tène decoration is similar to that of the tubular torc from Broighter (see page 101). 1st century BC.*

There was no likelihood that the chief of Tyrone would be in a position to unite the whole kingdom, but the statement nevertheless confirms his right to kingship. This is also emphasised by the description of his family name as "of the nine fetters", an allusion to his mythical ancestor, Niall of the Nine Hostages, who founded the O'Neill dynasty at about the time that chains for nine prisoners were being deposited at Llyn Cerrig Bach. The number, three times three, is undoubtedly significant for the Celts were very keen on the number three. Three-headed images are well known in Gaul and Ireland and both Irish and Welsh myth refer constantly to triads, triplets and triple events.

Contact with Rome

The Celtic fringe could not remain totally isolated from its conquered neighbours and Romanisation gradually had an effect throughout both of the islands. New technologies such as water power and literacy seem to have spread. There was some trade and late Roman silver has been found in both Scotland and Ireland. With trade came opportunities for raiding. Just as the Celts had moved into north Italy some five centuries earlier, so the Irish started to move into the edges of Roman Britain. Here they set up the Decies colonies in southwest Wales and the Dalriada colony in Argyll. At this time the Irish were known in Latin as the Scotti — Scotland takes its name and its Gaelic language from the Irish colony.

Christianity — A Roman Export

The major export from Roman Britain to the north and west was Christianity. The Irish acquired Christianity in the fifth century AD from their Welsh colonies, the Picts from a mission by St Ninian who was said to be a disciple of Martin of Tours.

◀ *Stone carving of a god with horns (or a horned helmet). He is holding a severed arm and may represent the mythical Nuadu whose arm, cut off in battle, was replaced by a silver one. From Tanderagee, co Armagh, Northern Ireland.*

Roman Britain was at that time Christian, as were all parts of the Roman Empire, but it was mostly famous for its support of the theologian Pelagius who had been declared a heretic in 418. Pelagius undermined the authority of the Church by rejecting the concept of original sin. Because his works were destroyed we do not know what exactly he thought or preached.

By 429, when St Germanus of Auxerre arrived from Gaul to flush out the last remnants of Pelagianism, Britain was in considerable turmoil. The Roman legionary army had been withdrawn to defend Gaul from Germanic incursions and Hadrian's Wall was abandoned. This left the Romano-British unprotected from their Celtic cousins, the Picts and Scots, who were raiding by sea.

The Anglo-Saxon Invasion

The Roman army gone, Britain called in Anglo-Saxon mercenaries from mainland Europe. This proved to be a terrible mistake for they soon turned upon their employers and many British made for lands beyond the sea. Some British refugees fled to the nearest Christian land, Brittany, where their language, mixed with a little Gaulish, survives today as Breton. Those Britons who remained went back to their traditional lifestyle, in some cases even refortifying the old Celtic hillforts.

The heroic ideal was revived with stirring tales of rebellion against the new Anglo-Saxon enemy, a rebellion led by the semi-mythical King Arthur. These stories have survived partly in the Welsh Mabinogi tales, partly in Breton literature.

◄Dún Aengus (fort of Angus), a massively defended clifftop fort overlooking the Atlantic on Inishmore, Aran Islands. The outer wall is surrounded by thousands of stones set on edge to repulse attackers. The existence of such a massive fortification on a site which is already almost inaccessible suggests not just a society of warriors, but one in which bigger was definitely better. The outer defenses, at the top of the picture, could be used to herd cattle in safety, while providing sufficient pasture.

◈ *The Gododdin* ◈

Now as in the past, however, the Celtic heroes were defeated. The Anglo-Saxon advance was as inexorable as the Roman had been, though much slower. The British struggles are recorded in the poems of two bards, Aneirin of Gododdin and Taliesin of Rheged. The Gododdin, or 'Votadini' as they were known in Latin, lived between the Roman Walls. The poem which commemorates them describes how 300 warriors rode out from Edinburgh to do battle with the Anglo-Saxons at Catraeth in North Yorkshire. They were totally defeated.

◄ *Pictish stone carved with horsemen, fighting animals, a centaur with an axe and the Christian symbol of Daniel in the lion's den. From Meigle, Scotland. 8th century AD. A Christian cross is carved on the other side of the stone.*

The Gododdin

From men who had been mead-nurtured
and wine-nurtured
a bright array charged forth, who had taken
sustenance together around the bowl.
For the feast in the mountain stronghold
they were to perish.
Too many have I lost of my true kinsmen.
Of the three hundred gold-torqued men who
attacked Catraeth,
alas! only one escaped.

The retinue of Gododdin from upon
rough-maned
horses the colour of swans with knotted
harness,
and in the first rank, leading the host in
the attack,
fighting for the groves and mead of Eidyn.
Because of the counsel of the mountain court,
shields had gone over;
blades had fallen
on white cheeks.
They loved fighting ... in the attack.
The men who would not flee bore no shame.

Islands of Saints, Scholars and Illuminated Manuscripts

A s the Roman Empire fell and western Europe plunged into chaos, Christianity became a major intellectual force. It introduced a whole new world of thought and knowledge to the Irish who, up until then, had seemed almost wilfully isolated. Perhaps news of the catastrophic events on the continent had reached them. More likely they were encouraged by the example of charismatic teachers like St Patrick, St Brigit or St Columba. At any event they now collected, copied and translated scores of Latin texts, which would otherwise be lost to us.

◁ *Becoming Scholars* ▷

At first glance, the Irish seemed unlikely saviours of academic knowledge, living as they did in an entirely rural environment, where wealth was counted in livestock, where society revolved around displays of vanity, and the value of a chief was measured by the amount of praise his poets could compose. They had no prior knowledge of mathematics nor of science beyond a fairly basic knowledge of astronomy. But

▶ *A title page from the Book of Kells, painted onto vellum, and showing a fantastic mingling of text and image. The right hand side of the frame is made up of a man's body whose legs can be seen in the bottom left hand corner.*

▼ *Skellig Michael, co. Kerry. A barren island in the Atlantic used as a monastery for Christian men fleeing the world to dedicate themselves to prayer and meditation.*

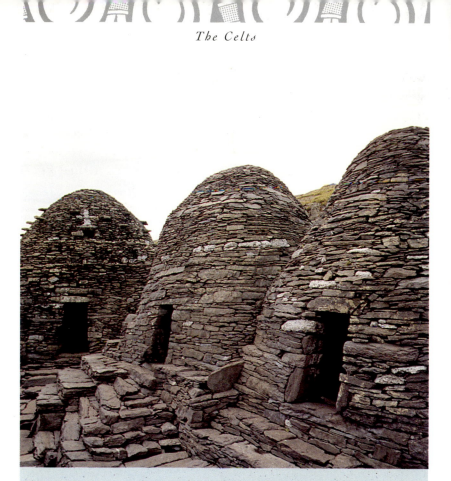

▲ *Monk's cells on Skellig Michael. The little beehive-shaped huts, made of unmortared stone, offered no creature comforts, and served only to exclude the frequent Atlantic gales. It is not clear what the monks might have lived on: water was widely available, but bread was not, nor was there much in the way of vegetation. They may have subsisted on lichens, shellfish, seaweed, and the occasional fish or gull's egg. 8th century AD*

scholarship could flourish in Ireland because there existed a learned class of poets, lawyers and druids, who were effectively subsidised to be intellectuals.

Their training consisted in memorising poetry and mythical stories. Many of these stories are not very different from those in the Bible upon

which Christianity was based and it is easy to see how the Christian story could appeal, simply as a story. But beyond the stories lies the religious explanation and it is here that the bardic and druidical training became unexpectedly useful. Part of the druids' function had been to advise the king on matters of law by drawing examples from their vast stock of stories. They were thus trained in analysis and also in the finer points of moral judgement.

Druids were greatly assisted in their new task by the acquisition of literacy. This was an innovation which they had apparently spurned earlier, as the Gaulish druids had done, for they preferred to keep their knowledge secret. The Christian preachers, on the other hand, were insisting that knowledge should be transmitted as widely as possible or souls would be damned. This must have been an extraordinarily radical idea to the more conservative druids and even to some of the new converts.

The point is made by the famous copyright case brought against St Columba by his teacher, who had been trained in the old druidical tradition. As a young student Columba was so eager to have his own copy of a book that he used to sneak into his teacher's study at night to copy the manuscript. The teacher successfully sued on the grounds that "to the cow belongs the calf" and therefore all copies of the manuscript belonged to its owner. A fine piece of logic, but hardly in the spirit of spreading the word of God.

By the seventh century the Irish clerics had not only mastered the reading and writing of Latin but they had also developed a means of writing down their own language. This required them to formulate laws of spelling without any prior information on the subject. They also analysed and wrote down the principles of Irish grammar, a peculiarly difficult task, since Irish and Latin have quite different grammatical systems. From then on the Irish clerics systematically collected and compiled information about their own society. As a result we have literally thousands of pages of manuscripts containing Irish poetry, law texts, glossaries, grammars, stories, saints' lives and chronicles of significant historical events.

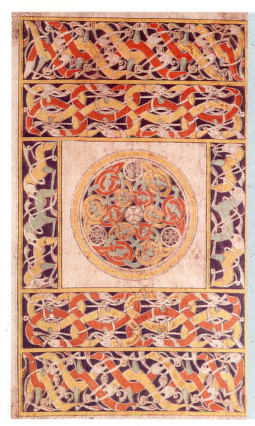

◀ *'Carpet page' from the* Book of Durrow, *folio 192v. This page shows the blending of Roman plaitwork and Anglo-Saxon animals in the insular style of manuscript illumination developed at Lindisfarne by Celtic and Anglo-Saxon scribes.*

▶ *Portrait of the evangelist Matthew painted onto parchment in the* Book of Durrow, *a gospel book for use in church ceremonies. The face is in distinctively Celtic style, with its staring eyes and comma-shaped curls. The interlace patterns on the border are borrowed from Roman mosaics, adapted to Celtic taste. 7th century AD.*

⚞ Truth and the Book ⚟

The Irish became obsessed with books. They read them, wrote them, carried them around in jewelled boxes, decorated them, copied their pictures onto stone crosses, and counted them as their most precious possessions. Books were thought to be in themselves holy and it became normal to use them for magical cures. They were carried into battle to ensure victory, they were dipped into cattle troughs to cure disease. Irish manuscripts survived the wave of destruction which accompanied the Protestant Reformation in the sixteenth century because they were hidden by their traditional owners, families who had for generations been entrusted with the care of these most venerated objects.

The reason for this book worship is that the Irish, like all the Celts, attached great importance to the spoken truth. The druids had held sway over the Gauls because they were the men of "true vision". Their word had been literally law. In Irish society the king held this power: if a king made a wrong judgement or lied, he and his kingdom were doomed. A good king, that is a truthful king, would bring health and life to all nature.

> *It is through the sovereign's truth that there may be plenty of*
> *every high, tall grain.*
> *It is through the sovereign's truth than an abundance of the*
> *water's fish swim upstream.*
> *It is through the sovereign's truth that fair offspring, borne of*
> *young women, are well begotten.*

How much more important then, they reasoned, would be the words of Christ, the greatest, the most truthful of kings.

Monasteries for Men and Women

There was one problem with book learning: it could no longer be stored in one's head, so the Irish had to reinvent the library. The scriptorium or writing house was an absolutely essential part of the monasteries where the clerics lived. These too were an innovation, though there already existed communal buildings for men, banqueting hostels and warriors' hall. There had not been communal houses for women, so female monasteries were a very considerable innovation. In a society dedicated to family, the idea that women might choose not to marry provoked intense conflict, particularly in the early days as St Patrick says:

> *There was a beautiful blessed noble-born Irishwoman whom I*
> *baptised; she received a prophecy from a divine messenger that*
> *she should become a virgin of Christ and draw nearer to God.*
> *Six days later she took the course that all virgins of God take,*
> *not with their father's consent but enduring the persecutions*
> *and deceitful hindrances of their parents. Nevertheless their*
> *number increases beyond counting.*

▶ *Silver and gold chalice from Derrynaflan. Part of a set of church plate found buried in a peatbog, probably in order to conceal it from Viking raiders. 9th century AD.*

▶ *Detail of chalice showing the exquisite workmanship of gold wire set in panels below the handle. The design is punctuated by studs of amber and enamel.*

▼ *The dish is edged with a fine silver tubular chain. The sides are made up of pressed metal panels with interlace and spiral designs, separated by rectangular plaques decorated with red, blue and yellow enamel.*

Monasticism was the perfect solution for a non-urban people coming to grips with a Christianity which had been developed in the major cities of the Empire. Fortunately both Patrick and the earlier missionaries from Wales had been trained in monasteries and could advise on their creation, but the Irish had a couple of problems: firstly, they had no rules of monastic conduct, so they devised their own, including an early form of confession; secondly, they could not acquire land on which to build, for in the Irish legal system land could not leave the family's ownership.

A compromise was reached whereby a local family would administer the monastery and so retain nominal ownership of the land. This is why abbots were frequently related to one another and how particular books or relics came to be cared for by particular families. One of the earliest known Irish manuscripts is a psalm book thought to have belonged to St Columba, but its name for centuries was *The Battle Book of the O'Donnells*, for they were relatives of Columba and carried his book into battle with them. It is a miracle that it has survived, but that should not surprise us, for it is Columba's job as a saint to work miracles.

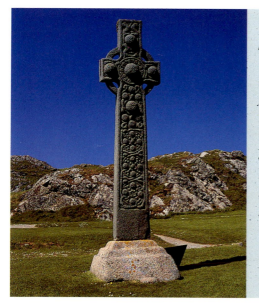

◀ St Martin's Cross at Iona, probably the earliest of the Celtic high crosses. The carving is of writhing snakes, a motif found throughout Scotland and Ireland. The snake symbolises the Christian resurrection, as it sheds its skin and is apparently reborn each year. As it had also been a pagan Celtic symbol, its use on a cross serves to show Christ's victory over paganism.

⊲ *Exiles for Christ* ⊳

Columba was the earliest of the Irish scholar-monks. He left his native Donegal in the sixth century to found a monastery at Iona in western Scotland on land belonging to his cousins, the local rulers. That monastery in turn founded others, all of which became centres of learning, concentrating particularly on training scribes and copyists. Lindisfarne, its offshoot in Anglo-Saxon Northumbria, was influential in consolidating Christianity there and in transmitting it to the Picts.

Also in the sixth century another Irish monk called Columbanus, in imitation of Columba, travelled to then pagan France and founded a series of monasteries in France, Switzerland and northern Italy. These too became centres of learning and from them spread a web of others through Germany, Austria and northern France. Each monastery had a library and a scriptorium in which manuscripts were copied and decorated in the characteristic "insular Celtic" style which reaches its highest point of beauty and craftsmanship in the *Great Gospel Book of Kells*.

As well as manuscripts the monasteries commissioned many other superb objects, chalices, brooches and reliquaries, manufactured by the descendants of those craftsmen who had in the past exalted Celtic chiefs and now exalted the King of Kings. The Picts, though in constant contact with both Iona and Lindisfarne, developed their own decorative styles, particularly in silver work. It is a great tragedy that no Pictish manuscripts at all have survived. Most would have been destroyed in the first wave of Viking attacks which swept down the east coast of Scotland towards the end of the eight century, destroying Lindisfarne in 792. The monks at Iona were more fortunate and were able to flee to Ireland with their precious relics in 801.

◀ *Page from the Gospel Book of Kells, showing a portrait of the evangelist St Matthew. He holds a gospel book in his left hand and is surrounded by the symbols of the other evangelists: the lion of St Mark, the calf of St Luke and the eagle of St John. Folio 28v.*

◀ *Silver bowl with punched ornament, part of a hoard found buried under a church at St Ninian's Isle, Shetland. 8th century AD.*

◀ *Silver cones from the St Ninian's hoard, each differently decorated with complex animal and spiral patterns. An internal fitting enables them to be threaded onto a strap and used as toggles or strap ends.*

◈ *Monastic Poets* ◈

The grandeur of the Church did not eclipse the Celts' love of nature and there is some wonderful poetry written by those hermits who had fled the world and its wealth:

> *The skilled lark calls,*
> *I go outside to watch it*
> *that I may see its gaping beak*
> *above against the dappled cloudy sky.*
> *I will sing my psalms*
> *for holy bright heaven*
> *that I may be shielded from harm*
> *for the purging of my sins.*

The monks in the scriptorium also wrote poems, this one to the monastery cat, Pangur, who can be seen frolicking in the pages of the *Book of Kells*:

> *I and my white Pangur*
> *Have each his special art:*
> *His mind is set on hunting mice*
> *Mine is upon my special craft.*
>
> *He points his full shining eye*
> *Against the fence of the wall:*
> *I point my clear though feeble eye*
> *Against the keenness of science.*
>
> *He rejoices with quick leaps*
> *When in his sharp claws sticks a mouse.*
> *I too rejoice when I have grasped*
> *A problem difficult and dearly loved.*

Women too wrote poems. This one is attributed to St Ita, who was miraculously given the baby Jesus to nurse:

> *Jesukin*
> *Is nursed by me in my little hermitage.*
> *All is a lie save Jesukin.*
>
> *A nursling that is nursed by me in my house,*
> *Jesu with men of heaven*
> *Before my heart every single night.*
>
> *Jesu noble, angelic*
> *Is nursed by me in my little hermitage.*
> *Jesu son of the Hebrew woman.*

❦ *Saints' Magic* ❦

While the monks were writing poems and learned treatises, the ordinary person, the man and woman in the field or hall, wanted more exciting stories. They were given these in an extraordinary outpouring of saints' lives and miracles, some of which are hardly Christian at all.

The Irish Christians had an ambiguous attitude to druids. The druids were obviously pagan, but they could do magical things which were very like the Christian miracles. The Irish Christians overcame this dilemma by having both Patrick and Columba engage in magical contests with the pagan king's druid. The saints always won, because their magic was beneficial: Patrick's opponent raised a snowstorm, but Patrick stopped the storm and brought back the sunshine.

Not all druids were regarded as evil and St Brigit, for instance, was educated by a druid, presumably one converted to Christianity. Magical stories abound of St Brigit, who was a real person, the illegitimate daughter of a serving girl. In pre-Christian times she would have been severely disadvantaged, since her inheritance would have been minimal and her marriage prospects poor. But she was able to radically change her status by taking advantage of the new opportunities. She founded a monastery for both men and women at Kildare in the sixth century AD and eclipsed Saint Patrick in popularity and influence for many centuries.

Brigit's name was that of a pagan goddess and a whole body of pagan folklore became transferred to her: it is said that on one occasion a column of fire rose from her head; another time that she willed the death of a bishop:

> *Condlaed was bishop of Kildare and he was devoured by wolves.*
> *This is the reason: he was Brigit's chief artist and tried to go to*
> *Rome in violation of Brigit's order. So Brigit prayed he might*
> *get a sudden death on his road and her prayer was fulfilled.*

In this story, Brigit is not behaving like a Christian, and certainly not like a saint. Nevertheless, she is so holy that even God will respect her wishes. Most of Brigit's miracles are rather more conventional, for instance,

▼ *Pictish bull-stone from the great fort of Burghead, Moray. Six of thirty such stones have survived. They were set into the wall of the citadel of the fort which guarded the northern coast of Scotland . 7th century AD.*

▶ *Flat silver plaque of unknown use from a hoard at Norries Law, Fife. The designs are the typically Pictish dog's head and Z rod symbol, combined with circles containing triple spirals. 7th century AD.*

multiplying loaves and making a cow give endless milk. One such miracle relates to the grant of land for her monastery: a landowner told her he would let her have as much land as her cloak could cover. The cloak miraculously grew to stretch over half a province, for Brigit was nothing if not practical.

Virgin Mothers

A peculiarity of saints is that they were miraculously born to saintly virgins. Ciaran was conceived when a star fell into the mouth of his sleeping mother; Finan when his mother bumped into a salmon as she was bathing; Boethine when his mother ate a nasturtium; Colman when his mother gave ink to a visiting monk. All of these miracles are direct echoes of Mary's miraculous conception of Jesus. Female saints are therefore strongly identified with the Mother of God, but they also reflect a Celtic preoccupation with goddesses. This is borne out by the portrayal of Mary as one of a set of three Marys:

> *The first Mary was the mother of our Lord Jesus Christ. The second Mary was the mother of the sons of Zebedee and she was the sister of the mother of our Lord. The third Mary was the mother of the sons of Alpheus and she too was the sister of the mother of our Lord.*

Patrick's family was even more miraculous, for he became credited with having five saintly sisters, one of whom was the mother of seventeen bishops and two abbesses. She presumably had not taken a vow of chastity.

These magical saints' lives are so earthy but also so innocent that they seem to reflect a genuine belief in the miraculous powers granted by God. While they seem to us occasionally grotesque or ludicrous they have to be seen in the perspective of a Celtic world in which reality was always elsewhere.

Many Irish regretted the passing of the heroes but thought of them as already having Christian virtues:

But how could the God you praise
and his mild priests singing a tune
Be better than Fionn the swordsman,
generous, faultless Fionn?

Just by the strength of their hand
The Fianna's battles were fought,
With never a spoken lie,
never a lie in thought.

The pagan ancestors had simply moved into that otherworld already inhabited by Ireland's mythical ancestors, the people of the Goddess. To Christ they attributed the powers formerly given to the king.

▶ *One of twenty carved stones from Meigle, Perth, probably from a monastic site. Over 250 such stones are known from eastern Scotland. They are carved with narrative scenes, Celtic crosses, and with the mysterious Pictish symbols: snakes, mirrors, mythical animals, Z and V rods. This one shows a chief on horseback, followed by a smaller figure, presumably his servant. Around them are Pictish symbols. 8th century AD.*

Peoples of the Goddess and the Parallel World of Faery

The Celtic world strove for harmony with nature and saw human beings as part of the continuum of creation. As the soul was eternal and could dwell as much in any part of nature as in human beings, the Celts did not separate humans from animals as sharply as modern Western society does. They perceived divinity in all aspects of the natural world, in trees, in rocks, in water, in all living things. They were well aware that as farmers, miners and sailors, they interfered with the natural order of things so had devised rituals designed to re-establish the balance through sacrifices which would give life back to nature. The often quoted "wicker man" ritual, which was used in times of extreme peril, is thought to have had the purpose of returning to nature the whole of creation. In this ritual, described by Caesar, many humans and different animals were placed together in a wicker enclosure shaped like a man and burnt alive.

The Great Queen

Nature was perceived as the primordial woman from whom were born all living things. She was not only a mother but also the queen of all creation. The Irish called her the Morrigán, the Great Queen. There is an early image of her from southeastern Austria, the Strettweg cart, a

▲ *A Celtic ritual cart. The scene represented is probably the hunting and sacrifice of stags (one at each end) for the goddess (shown in the centre). The bowl she holds above her head may have been intended to collect blood from a real stag sacrifice, or a symbolic liquid such as wine to represent blood. From Strettweg, Austria.*

bronze ritual cart found in a seventh-century BC tomb. Its centrepiece is a naked woman with strongly emphasised breasts and vulva, surrounded by much smaller figures of naked women, and horsemen armed with axes. At each end are stags with naked girls on either side. The figures are mounted on a four-wheeled platform decorated with horned animal heads. The larger woman holds a bronze bowl on her upraised hands. She is clearly a goddess of wild animals and of warfare. As goddess of the wild animals, she is like the Greek Artemis (Diana), who was worshipped by the Celtic Galatians; as goddess of war she is like the Gaulish Cathubodua and the Irish Badb.

Throughout the Celtic world there were only minimal shrines and few images of gods prior to the Roman conquest. But enough survives to show that female divinities far outnumbered male gods. It is worth

▲ *Details of the Strettweg cart. The base is an openwork plaque onto which the figures are bolted. The bowl is supported partly by the arms of the goddess and partly by crossed struts, twisted to resemble cables. The goddess is surrounded by horsemen who are naked but wear a pointed helmet and carry a short spear in the right hand and a shield in the left. In the right hand image, a young girl holds the stag's horns; behind her is a naked woman wearing earring; in the far right is the axe with which the stag will be sacrificed.*

recalling that one of the few things we know about the Galatians is the name of their goddess, Agdistis, which may be a Celtic name for Artemis (Diana). Since goddesses are the mothers of nature wild animals are far more commonly associated with goddesses than with male gods: horses with Epona, boars with Arduinna, bears with Artio, hounds with Nehalennia — only the stags are mainly associated with a male god, Cernunnos.

⚜ *A Thirst for Death* ⚜

Goddesses are strongly linked with death and had particularly bloody rituals. Boudicca was said to have sacrificed her Roman captives to the goddess Andraste by impaling them alive. Tacitus reports that on an island in the Atlantic Ocean, a shrouded image of the mother goddess

Nerthus was paraded from village to village on a four-wheeled cart then brought down to a lake where she was ritually washed by people who were immediately killed and thrown into the lake.

These ritual carts resemble the bronze model buried at Strettweg or the two wooden carts loaded with pots and part of a loom sunk into Dejberg pond in Denmark. These carts had been made in Gaul and elaborately decorated with bronze openwork designs: one has a ceremonial seat ideal for parading a goddess image. The loom may have served to weave her sacred shroud. The people who served the goddess would have been sanctified by their contact with her and death would be for them a reward, taking them to the otherworld to live in everlasting joy.

In Gaul we hear of an annual rite which involves the killing of a woman chosen at random. This differs from druidical practice as there is no executioner and no weapons: everybody kills the victim, probably to distribute the blood-guilt among all the participants to prevent feuding and revenge

The women were the Samnites who dwelt near the mouth of the Loire, on a coastal island

▶ *Epona, the Gaulish horse-goddess. To the Romans she was a patron of horseracing and cavalry men, but to the Celts she had wider significance as a goddess representing both power and death. Stone carving. 2nd century AD.*

▲ *Detail of a votive cart from Dejberg, Denmark. One of a pair which had been dismantled and sunk into a peatbog, the site marked by an encloure. The carts are of Gaulish manufacture and one is decorated with small bronze warrior heads with stiff hair and moustaches. 1st century BC.*

where no man was allowed to land. Each year they took the roof of their temple and put on a new one, in one day's work between dawn and sunset. If any woman dropped her burden she would be torn to pieces by the others howling in frenzy as they carried the dismembered body around the shrine. This happened every year, because each year somebody accidentally bumped into the woman who was doomed to die.

⪧ *Dolls and Witches* ⪦

Women's popular religion is quite well documented from Roman Gaul, because of the custom of placing images in healing wells to ask for a cure, or to give thanks for one. Most of these gifts are made by women and many represent women. In addition, little clay figurines, about 10 centimetres (4 inches) high, were mass-produced by the thousand for use in the home. The overwhelming majority of these, almost 90 per cent, were of women. The most popular was a water goddess, a semi-naked young woman whose drapery resembles falling water. The next most popular was the divine mother, shown as a woman almost covered with drapery and wearing an elaborate headdress. She is breastfeeding one or two very small children, the disparity in size indicating that she is a divine, not a human, mother.

▼ *Goddess with animals, shown on the inside of the Gundestrup Cauldron. The elephants and griffins are not Celtic, though the wolf might be. The wheel shapes have been interpreted as tambourines, with bells around their rim. 1st century BC.*

Women's daily religious practices were not always kindly. From southern France comes a letter written in Gaulish on a lead plaque and placed in a newly-dug grave near the mountain village of Larzac. The authors are two women who accuse nine of their neighbours of being witches. They ask the unnamed gods of the underworld to turn the witches' spells back against them. It is a chilling document, particularly because of the care with which it names the nine witches. The underground powers are clearly fearsome, for a hastily added postscript asks that they spare the innocent: "...do not be a spellcaster underground, under the new tombs of the people". The text, in speaking of the "magic of women", uses precisely the same words as are used in Ireland six centuries later. This goes beyond a coincidence and makes clear that there were common beliefs and a common religious vocabulary throughout the Celtic world.

Brigit — Saint and Goddess

A great deal of information about myth was preserved in Ireland, where the Christian writers were very interested in their pagan past. They wrote down many stories to which they added elaborate explanations about the events and people concerned. In the ninth century AD King Cormac of Cashel even compiled a glossary which is quite specific about goddesses. The most famous was probably the triple goddess Brigit:

> *This is Brigit the female seer or woman of insight, the goddess whom the poets used to worship, for her cult was very great and splendid. Her sisters were Brigit the woman of leechcraft and Brigit the woman of smithcraft. Goddesses, the three daughters of the Dagdae are they.*

These Brigits are essentially creators and healers. In the historic period there was a Saint Brigit, the abbess of the great double monastery of Kildare. So many miraculous stories are told about her that scholars think the old worship of the goddesses was simply transferred to the saint. This seems very likely, for many wells are named after St Brigit, even in England where they are called Bridewell, but there are no stories associating the historic St Brigit with any wells. It has also been

▲ *Gold torc and matching bracelets from a tomb at Waldalgesheim, Germany. The wooden chamber contained a war-chariot and a banquet service, though no body was recovered. The tomb is thought to be that of a woman. 3rd century BC.*

▶ *Tubular gold torc from southern France, the sort of object that might be given as an offering to a female god. 3rd century BC.*

noticed that the name Kildare means "church of the oak tree", that St Brigit was educated by a druid, and that druids were much associated with oak trees. St Brigit may well have deliberately emphasised pagan ritual in order to place Christian worship in a familiar context.

A more surprising survival is that of the great goddess identified in Irish sources as Danu or Anu which *Cormac's Glossary* describes as: "Anu: the mother of the gods of the Irish. She nurtured well the gods." This goddess lived on into Christian times in the guise of the Sainte Anne worshipped throughout Brittany, particularly at wells and on seashores.

Entering the Otherworld

Anu's people, the Tuatha Dé Danaan, or people of the goddess, had been driven underground by the ancestors of the historical Irish, but appeared from time to time to chosen heroes. We know little about that other world, which the British sometimes called Avalon and the Irish Tir na nOg, the land of everlasting youth. It could be entered by special heroes like Pwyll, Lord of Dyfed, who changed places for a year with Arawn, king of the otherworld kingdom of Annwyn. Pwyll returned to Dyfed to find that Arawn had made his land more prosperous and happy than it had ever been. But Oisin, who spent a year in Tir na nOg, had a less happy homecoming, for in that place a year passed in a day and a century in a year. So on Oisin's return he found that all his comrades had died and he himself was now an old man in a changed world.

The mother goddess was explicitly identified with the land of Ireland. For instance, in *The Book Of Invasions*, compiled in the twelfth century from older material, the great druid Amergin prays to Ireland to receive his people, the ancestors of the historic Irish: "I invoke the land of Ireland, the great lady Ireland." Thereafter kingship was given only to those men whom the local goddess chose to marry, so kingship effectively came from the union between man and nature, personified by the regional goddess who often had a triple personality: ruler, woman and mother.

The Three Machas

The great ritual sites were named after the goddesses. Ruling families sought to associate themselves with them, occasionally through the device of a ritual marriage, even in the Christian period. The stories were adjusted over time to suit different dynastic claims, so that there are many variations on one theme; but we can take the story of the three Machas as an example.

The first Macha was the wife of Nemed who settled Ireland before the Tuatha Dé and had cleared the forests to make twelve plains fit for grazing. He gave one to Macha, that it might bear her name. She died there.

Macha the Red was the only child of King Aed, who reigned jointly with his two brothers, each one ruling for seven years in turn. When Aed died, leaving his share to Macha, his brothers refused to let a woman rule them, but Macha defeated them in battles and ruled for seven years. At the end of that time one of her two uncles died, leaving five sons, who now claimed the kingship. But she defeated them too in battle, then married her remaining uncle, making him the chief of her army.

She then disguised herself as a leper and went into the forest where her five cousins had taken refuge. The first led her away and tried to rape her, but she overcame him, tied him up and returned to the others. Each in turn took her into the forest and each in turn was overcome. Then she took them back with her to the plain of Macha and forced them to build the royal site of Macha.

The third Macha was a beautiful woman of the otherworld who came one day into the house of a rich widower named Crunnchu. She never spoke but tidied the house, cooked food then went to his bed. When King Conor held his annual horse race,

► *Small bronze plaque which is 9.5 cm (3¾ inches) high, from the tomb at Waldalgesheim. It shows a goddess with raised hands. She wears a torc and her upper arms and torso are covered with curving tattoos or bodypaint.*

Crunnchu boasted his wife could outrun the king's horses. Macha pleaded that she was about to give birth but Conor insisted that she run. She won the race, but died at its end, while giving birth to twins (Emain), whence the name Emain Macha. As she died she cursed Conor and his descendants.

The three stories each intersect to show that Emain Macha is a royal place and the last one explains why it was destroyed. But they also show the diversity of roles the Celtic goddess might play: Macha is beautiful, a good housekeeper and concerned mother, but she is also a great and cunning warrior.

❧ *Fairy Women* ❧

The same qualities are evident in the Welsh story of Rhiannon ("queen") who lures Pwyll of Dyfed into marriage.

Pwyll of Dyfed was hunting and saw a beautiful woman ride in front of him at a slow walk. He tried to catch up with her, but couldn't reach her however fast he galloped. This happened three nights in a row until he called out to her: "Stop, for the sake of the man you love." She stopped then and told him he was the one she loved, but that she was engaged to marry another. Pwyll agreed to dispose of this unwanted lover, following Rhiannon's instructions. This took three years to carry out and involved elaborate deceit and some cruelty. Finally Pwyll and Rhiannon were married but her child was stolen from her by evil forces. At the end of seven years the child was miraculously returned. He became a great king when his father died. Rhiannon went back to the otherworld and married the god of the sea, Manawydan son of Llyr, or Manannán mac Lir as he is known in Irish.

This is a story intended to legitimate kingship by connecting the dynasty to a divine mother. Like the Machas, Rhiannon is young, beautiful and a loving mother, but she is also ruthless and cunning. There are many similar stories, most of which involve a woman who is ugly but becomes beautiful when the future king treats her with courtesy. The idea is that the ugly woman represents the land withered by a bad king; when the right man becomes king, the land blooms again.

To find such a woman the hero had to enter the otherworld. This could be reached at any time, but was particularly close to humans during the four feast days of the Celtic year, which correspond very approximately to the seasons of a farming year. They start in winter with Samain (1st of November), followed by Imbolc, the lambing day (1st of February), spring or Beltaine (1st of May) and the midsummer feast of Lughnasad (1st of August). On those days, fires were lit at the festival places, there were games and markets, betrothals arranged and weddings celebrated, disputes were settled and contracts renewed. It was at Samain that the hero Cúchulainn was lured to the síd by a vision of the fairy Fann, though in reality he was lying in a deathly trance in his wife's home.

These feast days have survived in folklore along with stories of the dangers of these nights. Memories of the mother goddesses survive in the tales of beautiful girls and mermaids who lure young men to their death, or steal new-born babies replacing them with impish changelings. These stories come from an ancient and fabulous world in which everything was possible, in which fame and fortune and love were within the grasp of any one brave enough to enter the world of the síd and its ever-golden youth.

▶ *Small bronze figurine of a Gaulish woman wearing a torc. She could be a goddess or one of the mythic enchantresses so popular in Celtic stories. 1st century AD.*

Fated Lovers

I n the Celtic world, bards would entertain the company in the king or queen's hall with tales of adventure and magic. There were various sorts of stories for different circumstances and bards had to know a selection for every occasion: battles, cattle raids, deaths, abductions, elopements and wooings. The skilful bard could improvise links between the stories which would flatter his host and the guests, by varying the local content or making some subtle compliment to the hostess.

While these stories are about mythical people, their settings are homely scenes of daily life and it is not difficult to accept that boys and girls did flirt on the green, or that mothers encouraged their daughters to follow their fancy.

Enchanting Girls

Wooings were enormously popular and many have survived to this day as folk stories. Some, much modified, have become part of mainstream European literature, such as the Arthurian Tales and the story of Tristan and Isolde. In all of these stories the heroine is beautiful and doomed. Even if she manages to marry the man of her choice, some tragedy will befall them. The tales are quite amoral, both men and women behaving in ways which flout all the conventions of their society, and for which they are inevitably punished — hence the tragic endings.

The texts often follow set literary patterns, so the description opposite of a heroine, the fairy Etain, used elements taken from Gallo-Roman poetry. It is noticeable that the Celtic woman, like the Japanese heroines of the *Tale of Gengi*, impresses because of the beauty of her clothes and jewels. This fits with everything we have seen of the Celtic love of show.

Wooing of Etain

Etain was a fairy, the most beautiful creature in Creation, who was loved throughout eternity and through successive reincarnations by the king of the fairies, Midir. Etain fell in love with the mortal king, Eochaid, and lived with him until his death. During this time, King Midir stole her away and hid her in the hills of the síd — fairyland; but Eochaid, at great risk to himself, brought her back to Tara. Etain is regarded as the archetypal personification of reincarnation.

King Eochaid of Tara was going across the green of Bri Leith when he saw a woman at the edge of a well. She was washing a bright comb of silver and gold in a silver basin which had four golden birds on it and little bright purple stones set in its rim. A beautiful purple cloak fringed by silver and held by a gold brooch was about her. Her dress was of green silk with a long hood embroidered in red gold. Wonderful clasps of gold and silver were on her breasts and on her shoulders and sunlight shimmered on the gold and the green silk. Her hair was in two plaits, four locks in each plait, a bead at the point of every lock. The colour of her hair was like yellow irises in summer, or like red gold after it is polished.

As she let her hair down to wash it, her arms came out from the sleeves of her dress. Her eyes were as blue as cornflowers, her lips as red as berries, and her body was like the foam of a wave. Her face glowed like the bright light of the moon, pride was in her eyebrows, and a dimple of delight was in each of her cheeks. The light of wooing was in her eyes, and when she walked she had a step that was steady and even, like the walk of a queen.

Of all the women of the world, she was the best and the most beautiful that had ever been seen, and she was, as King Eochaid and his people thought, from the hills of the síd. It is of her it was said: "All are dear and all are shapely till they are put beside Etain."

When Cúchulainn meets Emer

The hero of the great epic, the Táin or Cattle-Raid of Cooley is Cúchulainn, nephew of King Conor mac Nes. He is a sprightly young lad who is irresistible to women though he loves only his wife Emer. In this account of their first meeting, Emer seems to have been very bold.

Emer was out on the playing field with her companions, the daughters of landowners who lived around Forgall's fort. She was teaching the girls needlework and fine embroidery. Cúchulainn came by on his chariot and greeted the girls. Emer lifted up her lovely face. Of all the young girls in Ireland, she was the one Cúchulainn thought the most desirable, for she had the six gifts: the gift of beauty, the gift of voice, the gift of sweet speech, the gift of needlework, the gift of wisdom, the gift of chastity. And Cúchulainn had said that no woman should marry him unless she was his equal in age, in appearance, in skill and handiness; she would also be the best worker with her needle of the young girls of Ireland. And that is why it was Emer he went to ask above all others.

Emer had recognised the hero and said, "May your way be blessed!" "May you see only good," he replied. Then they spoke together in riddles. While they were talking like this, Cúchulainn saw the maiden's breasts over the top of her dress. "Fair is this plain, the plain of the noble yoke." And Emer said, "No one comes to this plain who does not overcome as many as a hundred men on each ford, from Ailbine to Banchuig Arcait." "As you have commanded, it will be done by me," said Cúchulainn. ▩

Kings and Heroes

A moral content in the stories illuminates the workings of Celtic society. This can be seen in the way the men are portrayed. They are quick to anger, loyal to their chief, troubled by wanton women, frightened by druids, saints and otherworld beings. The stories describe the consequences of their actions and the ultimate message is probably that men should give more thought to their behaviour.

A theme running throughout Celtic stories is that of the older man, usually a highly loved and respected king, who desires a beautiful young girl. But the girl loves a handsome young man — her natural mate — who risks everything for her love. The older man will not give up and in the wake of his obsession, tragedy follows.

In the story *Deirdre of the Sorrows*, had Conor mac Nes reflected on the prophecy surrounding the birth of Deirdre, he would have known he should not think of her as a future bride. He creates problems for himself and for his kingdom because he is trying to defy the laws of nature and also those of society. He tries to overcome age by marrying a much younger woman without consulting her. Worse, he flouts all the normal marriage arrangements by failing to negotiate with the kin: Deirdre is taken away from her family at birth and fostered by parents of Conor's choosing. Conor is punished, not because of his foolish lust, but because he has subverted the social order. In so doing he has lost the magical power of the good king. In his reign there will be death, not life, and waste instead of fertility. The story is therefore a powerfully moral one, driving home the message that the life of the individual must give way to the good of the greater number.

Deirdre of the Sorrows

*The greatest of all Celtic love stories is that of
Deirdre and the sons of Uisliu. As in the Tristan, Isolde
and Mark triangle, this is a story in which an older
man, King Conor mac Nes covets a beautiful young
girl, Deirdre. The story of Deirdre can be seen as a
Christian attack on sexual lust, both Conor's for Deirdre
and Deirdre's for Noisiu, but it is also a profoundly
moving story of adolescents caught up in the world of
adult intrigue.*

While King Conor mac Nes was feasting with the heroes of the
Red Branch at the house of Felim the bard, a cry was heard
from their hostess's womb. The druid Cathbad declared the child
would be called Deirdre, which means sorrow. When the child was
born, Cathbad prophesied that she would become the loveliest of
women, but that her beauty would bring evil and ruin upon
Ireland. His followers wished to kill the child, but Conor resolved
to bring the child up to be his bride. He kept her in seclusion from
all but a few servants and a mischievous poet. For sixteen years,
Deirdre lived in solitude, a prisoner in the dark forest with no one
for company but old men and women. Only Conor hunted these
forests, death being the penalty for anyone trespassing.

One day she and her companion the poet watched her foster
mother killing a calf. A raven flew down to pick at the crimson
blood on the fresh snow. Deirdre said, "I could love a man whose
skin was white as snow, whose cheeks were as red as blood, whose
hair was as black as the raven."

"Noisiu, Uisliu's son, is one like that," the poet said. "And so are Ainnle and Ardan, his two brothers. The colour of the raven is on their hair, their skin is like the swan on the wave, their cheeks like the blood of the speckled red calf, and their swiftness and their leap are like the salmon of the stream and the deer of the mountain. And the head and shoulder of Noisiu are above all the other men of Ireland."

"I saw them last night in a dream," said Deirdre, "and they were hunting on a hill."

"He's not too far away," the poet said.

Deirdre watched out for Noisiu and recognised him at once. She quickly went out and made as though she did not see him. His horse stopped, refusing to pass her, and Noisiu thought her not mortal. Deirdre loved him with her soul and body. She touched his horse and Noisiu loved her too. Deirdre begged him to take her away with him, but virtuous Noisiu refused to be tempted, knowing the commands of the king. Deirdre threatened to shame him publicly if he didn't go away with her, so he and his two brothers left with their warriors and their women, and took to a life of exile. Though they kept Deirdre hidden, everywhere they went news of her beauty spread and conflict was created.

King Conor mac Nes could not forget Deirdre and the three brothers. He thought of her with love and of the brothers with hate. Finally, after many years, he sent for them all to return, swearing he would not harm them. He broke his word and the brothers and all their entourage were killed leaving only Deirdre to lament over Noisiu. When Deirdre still refused him, Conor threatened to give her in marriage to Noisiu's killer, so she jumped from her chariot dashing her brains out against a rock.

Tristan and Isolde

If young love was considered with approbation by the audience, adultery was even more thrilling, particularly if the lovers could not help their fate. The greatest of all these stories is that of Tristan and Isolde, originally a Pictish story involving Drustan who was in love with Essylt, wife of Mark whose territory Drustan was guarding from the attacks of Arthur. All of these characters became very much changed when the story was adopted by Breton and Welsh writers and included in the Arthurian tales, chivalric tales in which the knight's oath of fealty to his lord is supposed to override all else.

Moraunt, the Queen of Ireland's brother, arrived at the court of King Mark of Cornwall demanding tribute. Tristan, the king's nephew, offered to fight the battle for Cornwall. He was wounded, but Tristan wounded Moraunt so badly that he later died. Moraunt's lance was poisoned, and Tristan became ill. He set sail for help in another kingdom, but his boat was driven by storms to Ireland. The King of Ireland and his daughter Isolde saw him playing his lute and sent for him. Isolde devoted herself to him, soon restoring him to health. It was discovered that it was Tristan who had killed the queen's brother. The queen demanded vengeance but the court declared that he should be sent home never to return.

Mark became intrigued by Tristan's description of Isolde. He ordered his nephew back to Ireland to obtain Isolde to be his queen. Bound by his oath, Tristan embarked for Ireland. Thrown off course by storms, Tristan found himself at Camelot where he helped clear the King of Ireland of charges against Arthur. In gratitude the King of Ireland offered Tristan any boon. They returned to Ireland together and with trembling voice Tristan demanded Isolde for his uncle, the King of Cornwall. The queen asked Isolde's maid to administer a love potion to Isolde and Mark. But on the ship, the maid gave Isolde and Tristan the love potion instead.

Isolde and Mark were married, but in an act of knightly honour, Mark lost Isolde to Sir Palamedes. Tristan recovered Isolde and they lived in the forest briefly before Tristan restored her to Mark. Mark, full of jealousy of his nephew, nearly killed Tristan. Tristan was banished and Isolde locked up in a tower. After many years and many adventures, Tristan aided King Hoel of Brittany in a war. In gratitude, Hoel offered Tristan his daughter, Isolde of the White Hands, in marriage. Tristan's love for Isolde the Fair was hopeless and it seemed as though destiny had provided Isolde of the White Hands for his happiness. Tristan grew more in love with his wife as time passed. The war broke out again and Tristan was severely injured. His wife tried to cure him but Tristan became weaker. Isolde of the White Hands consented to Isolde the Fair being sent for since her ministrations had cured him before. Tristan asked the servant that if the Queen of Cornwall returned with him to put up white sails; that if she refused put up black sails. When Isolde of the White Hands learned of the previous love between Tristan and the Queen of Cornwall, she directed that Tristan be told the returning ship bore black sails. In grief Tristan died. Isolde the Fair arrived too late and expired holding Tristan in her arms. Their bodies were returned to Cornwall where a sorrowful King Mark had them buried side by side with a vine on Tristan's grave and a rose on Isolde's. The plants grew inextricably intertwined. 🔲

The Druid's Prophecy

At the heart of Celtic stories is the playing out of the tragedy foretold by the druid. It is a constant theme that the druid's prophecies always come true.

Stories often start with the question to the druid: what is this day good for? His answer then determines the rest of the action as the heroine attempt to fulfil the prophecy, as in the story of the conception of King Conor mac Nes.

Nes, the daughter of Eochu of the Yellow Heel, was sitting with her attendants outside her home, Emain Macha, when the druid Cathbad came by. She asked him what the hour was good for, and he replied: "For begetting a king on a queen." Then he told her that a son conceived in that hour would be known throughout Ireland forevermore. As no other man was nearby, she invited the druid into the house. A child was conceived who then stayed in her womb for three years and three months. As the birth time nears, Nes takes some rather painful precautions to ensure that he is born at the most auspicious moment — she sits on a rock in mid-river to delay the birth. When he is eventually born, she intrigues to make him king, though he is not entitled to it. As each wrong action is eventually punished, Conor ultimately pays the price of his mother's wrongdoing and of his own misdeeds. His people are plunged into war and Emain Macha is destroyed. The story of this war is told in the great epic, the *Táin* or *Cattle-Raid of Cooley*.

The Story is in the Telling

There are innumerable side stories and episodes around each main plot which every story teller would have embroidered appropriately. The most prized quality of such stories is loyalty to the loved one, though this does not necessarily entail fidelity. The main themes are illustrated well in both the Deirdre and Tristan and Isolde stories: the woman doomed by her beauty, the reluctant lover — for neither hero wishes to betray his king — the stay in the forest, the obstinate king. These elements are also in another Irish story: The Pursuit of Diarmaid and

Grainne, in which Grainne, wife of the hero Fionn, bewitches Diarmaid into eloping with her. Grainne threatens Diarmaid with spells of danger and destruction if he does not take her away with him. They flee and are pursued throughout Ireland, where many place names still commemorate them, until they finally die.

In all of these stories, while entertainment value was probably high, there was also an overtly political content, largely intended to boost the prestige of whichever patron had commissioned the performance. When the stories were written down, this variation was no longer possible, so the scribes went to some lengths to try and make them relevant to their time by adding explanations or relevant geographical and historical material. As a result they are an astonishingly rich source of information about Celtic society and psychology, and there is an ever growing body of scholarship around them.

For most of us, however, the stories are memorable in themselves, for the richness of the settings, for the courage of the characters, particularly the women, and for the sheer romance of love and beauty pitted against the mean-minded world. In modern times they have been a source of inspiration for artists as diverse as Wagner, Tennyson, the Pre-Raphaelite painters, W.B. Yeats, James Joyce and Seamus Heaney.

◄ The Celts' love of words and story telling is reflected in the enduring myths of King Arthur. These tales give a marvellous insight into Celtic mysticism, their love of beauty and devotion to honour and heroic deeds. Here is Tintagel Castle, reputed to be the birthplace of King Arthur.

Picture Credits

Ancient Art and Architecture Collection

Front and back cover background – Beginning of summary of Gospel of Matthew, folio 8r, Book of Kells
Back cover and p. 27B – Greek bronze vessel from Vix, Hallstatt
Endpapers – Eight Circle Cross, Gospel of St Matthew, Book of Kells
p. 22B, p. 30, p. 34, p. 37, p. 39, p. 45, p. 48, p. 62A, p. 105, p. 113A, p. 119A, p. 129

Artephot

p. 40A (Artephot/M.E. Boucher), p. 40B (Artephot/M.E. Boucher), p. 64 (Artephot/Trela), p. 68B (Artephot/Nimatallah), p. 81B (Percheron/Artephot), p. 86 (Artephot/Baguzzi)

British Museum, London

p. 102 (copyright British Museum)

Ch.Thioc/Musée de la Civilization gallo-romaine, Lyon – Conseil Général du Rhône

p. 57

Peter Clayton

p. 25 , p. 139

CM Dixon

Front cover and p. 29 – detail of silver cauldron from Gundestrup
Front cover and p. 25 – Tara brooch
p. 12, p. 14, p. 23, p. 26, p. 59, p. 67, p. 72, p. 77, p. 71, p. 81A, p. 85, p. 90, p. 94, p. 97, p. 102, p. 119B, p. 119C, p. 125A, p. 125B, p. 127, p. 131, p. 132, p. 133

Aedeen Cremin

p. 10, p. 82

Department of the Environment for Northern Ireland, Belfast

p. 103

Robert Estall Photo Library

p. 95, p. 111

e.t. archive

p. 21, p. 122A

Foto WIROBAL/Museum Hallstatt

p. 13

Giraudon

p. 18 (Lauros-Giraudon), p. 19 (Lauros-Giraudon), p. 20, p. 22C, p. 28B (Lauros-Giraudon), p. 41 (Lauros-Giraudon), p. 42 (Lauros-Giraudon), p. 43, p. 44A (Lauros-Giraudon), p. 44B (Lauros-Giraudon), p. 47, p. 58 (Lauros-Giraudon), p. 61A (Lauros-Giraudon), p. 61B (Lauros-Giraudon), p. 62B (Lauros-Giraudon), p. 91 (Lauros-Giraudon), p. 93 (Lauros-Giraudon), p. 135B (Lauros-Giraudon)

Landesmuseum Joanneum, Graz, Austria

p. 130A/B

Ian Jack

p. 17, p. 66

Magyar Nemjeti Museum

p. 74

Moravian Museum, Brno, Czech Republic

p. 75

Museé de Cluny, Paris

(© photo RMN)

p. 87, p. 88, p. 92A/B

Museé du Châtillonais, Châtillon-sur-Seine, France

p. 27A

Museo Civico Romano, Brescia, Italy

p. 60

Museo Numantino, Soria, Spain

p. 50

Narodnija Archeologiceski Muzej, Sofia

p. 76A/B

National Museum of Copenhagen, Denmark

p. 28A

National Museum of Ireland, Dublin

Back cover and p. 101A – gold tubular torc from Broighter, co. Derry, p. 101B

National Museum of Scotland, Edinburgh

p. 96, p. 98, p. 99, p. 122A, p. 122B

Naturhistorisches Museum, Vienna

p. 15, p. 73A/B/C

Further Reading

General

Aedeen Cremin, *The Celts in Europe* (Sydney University Centre for Celtic Studies 1992)

Christiane Eluère, *The Celts: First Masters of Europe* (Thames & Hudson 1993)

Miranda Green, ed. *The Celtic World* (Routledge 1995)

Simon James, *Exploring the World of the Celts* (Thames & Hudson 1993)

John Koch and John Carey, *The Celtic Heroic Age: Literary Sources for Ancient Celtic Europe and Early Ireland and Wales* (Celtic Studies Publications, Malden, Mass. 1995)

Art and Archeology

Venceslas Kruta et al. eds, *The Celts* (Thames & Hudson 1991).

Ruth and Vincent Megaw, *Celtic Art from its Beginnings to the Book of Kells* (Thames & Hudson 1989)

Bernard Meehan, *The Book of Kells* (Thames & Hudson 1995)

Classical Authors

H.D. Rankin, *Celts and the Classical World* (Croom Helm 1987)

Appian's Roman History, trans. H. White (Heinemann 1928)

Caesar, The Battle for Gaul, trans. A. & P. Wiseman (Chatto & Windus 1980)

Livy: The Early History of Rome, trans. A. de Selincourt (Penguin 1960)

Polybius: the Rise of the Roman Empire, trans. I. Scott-Kilvert (Penguin 1979)

Tacitus, The Annals of Imperial Rome, trans. M. Grant (Penguin 1956)

Tacitus, On Britain and Germany, trans. H. Mattingly (Penguin 1948)

Boudicca

Antonia Fraser, *Boadicea's Chariot: The Warrior Queens* (Weidenfeld and Nicholson 1988).

Druids

Nora Chadwick, *The Druids* (University of Wales 1966)

Lindow Man

Don Brothwell, *The Bog Man and the Archeology of People* (British Museum 1986)

Mythology

Miranda Green, *Dictionary of Celtic Myth and Legend* (Thames & Hudson 1992)

Ireland

Barry Raftery, *Pagan Celtic Ireland: the Enigma of the Iron Age* (Thames & Hudson 1994)

Michael Richter, *Medieval Ireland* (Gill & Macmillan 1988)

Fergus Kelly, *A Guide to Early Irish Law* (Dublin Institute of Advanced Studies 1988).

Celtic Poetry and Stories

The Gododdin, version by D. O'Grady (Dolmen 1977)

The Táin, trans. Thomas Kinsella (Dolmen 1969)

Jeffrey Gantz, *Early Irish Myths and Sagas* (Penguin 1981)

Frank O'Connor, *Kings, Lords and Commons* (Macmillan 1961)

Jeffrey Gantz, *The Mabinogion* (Penguin 1976)

The Mabinogion, trans. G. and T. Jones, (Everyman's Library revised ed.1993)

Sources of translations used in this book

John Koch and John Carey, *The Celtic Heroic Age: Literary Sources for Ancient Celtic Europe and Early Ireland and Wales* (Celtic Studies Publications, Malden, Mass. 1995)

Lady Gregory, *Cuchulainn of Muirthemne: the Story of the Men of the Red Branch of Ulster* (John Murray 1902)

Kate MacLeod, *The Participation of Women in Land-Related Conflicts*, unpublished MA thesis in Celtic Studies, University of Sydney 1992

Kuno Meyer translations, quoted in Nora Chadwick, *The Celts* (Penguin 1970)

Whitley Stokes, *Féilire Oengusso* (Henry Bradshaw Society 29, 1905)

Index

Page references in *italic*
type indicate illustrations.

afterlife 54, *61*
Agdistis (goddess) 130
agriculture 13
Alexander the Great 76–77
Aneirin of Gododdin 110
Anglesey (Britain) 55,
    98–100
Anglo-Saxon invasion of
    Britain 109–111
Ankara (Turkey) 78
Antonine Wall
    (Britain) 97
Anu (goddess) 134–135
architecture 17
art
    see also sculptures; vessels
    development 19–22
    warriors in *39,* 39–40
Arthur, King 109, *149*
Austria
    colonisation 75, 80
    tombs 23

banquets 42
bards 16, 19, 42, 52, *53,*
    140–149
bedding 17
bodyguards 43
Bohemia 14, 75
Boii people 78–79
Bolgios 77
Book of Durrow *116–117*
Book of Kells *113, 122*
books *113,* 116–117,
    116–118, *122*
Bosnia 80
Bosphorus 78
Boudicca of the Iceni
    24–26, 130
bracelets *18, 63*
Brennos 78
Breton language 12

Brigantes 24
Brigit, St 124–126,
    134–135
Britain 96–100
    Anglo-Saxon mercenaries
        109–111
    Christianity 107–109
    Gallo-Roman religion
        95, *95*
    jewellery 26, 96–97
    language 9, 12, 96
    Roman colony 89
    Romanisation 90
    warfare 52
    warrior queens 24
Brittany 14, 97
bronze
    ornaments *19, 22, 97,*
        102, 137
    sculpture *58*
    vase *27*
    vessels *42*
    weapons *20–21*
brooches *31, 35, 37*
Bulgaria 75, 80
burial 23, *23*
    women 27

Caesar 87–89, 97–98
Caledonians 96
calendar 56–57, *57, 139*
Caratacus of the
    Catuvellauni 24
Carthage 84
Carthaginians 79
Cartimandua of the
    Brigantes 24
Celtiberians
    language 9, 12
    Roman conquest 84
    weapons 48
Celtica 9, 9–10
chalice *119*
challenge 39
champions 43

chariot fighting 45–46
chariots *38, 44–46, 76*
chiefs
    banquets 42
    bodyguard 43
    sculpture *51*
    tombs 41–42
    war 52
children 18, 33
Christianity
    Britain 107–109
    introduction 95
    Ireland 107–109,
        112–127, *113–127*
Cisalpine Celts 78
cities 74
clothing
    Roman-style 93
    women 28–29, *28–29*
coins 19, *38, 49, 68, 76, 87*
Coligny calendar 57, *57*
Columba, St 115, 120–121,
    124
Columbanus 121
commerce *see* trade
cooking 17
Cornwall
    language 12
    mining 14
courage 38, 43, 77, 79
crafts *see* art
"crofters' war" (Scotland) 37
crosses *120*
Cúchulainn 38, *142*

Dacian people 73
Danu (goddess) 134–135
Danube valley *73,* 75–76,
    79–80
death
    after life 54
    religious rituals 130–132
death masks *62*
decorative art *19, 20,*
    20–21, 29, 37

Deidre 143–145, 148
Delphi (Greece) *71, 77, 78*
diet 13
divorce 32–33
dowry 31
druids 54–69
  abolition 91
  Britain 98–100
  Christianity in Ireland
    115, 124
  cultural custodians 19, 69
  medicine 68–69
  in stories 148
  training 55–56
  war 55
Dying Gaul (sculpture)
  80,81

earrings *18*
economy 19
education 18
Emain Macha (Ireland) *103,*
  103–104
Empire, Gallic 94
enamel *20, 46*
England 97
Epona *131*
Etruscans
  artistic influence 19
  Celtic settlement 72, 74
  trade 23
extended families 18

fairy-folk 102
  women 138–139
family life 18–19
fidelity 34
fighting *see* war; warriors
figurines 133
fortifications 108
  "oppida" 16–17, *17*, 76
fosterage 33
France *see* Gaul

Gaelic language *9*, 12, 101
Galatia 78, *79*
Galician language 12
Gallia Cisalpina 71
Gallic Empire 94

Gaul
  druids 55
  human sacrifice 131–132
  images of the otherworld
    66
  language *9, 12*
  monasteries 121
  represented by woman's
    head *25*
  Roman colony *88, 89*
  Roman conquest *85,*
    85–89
  Romanisation 93–94
  sacred spring 67
  trophy heads 61
generosity 8
goddesses 128–138,
  129–133, 137, 139
Gododdin (poem) 52,
  110–111
gods 63
  Ireland *106*
  under the Romans 91–93
  sculpture *62, 65, 93, 106*
gold
  mining 14
  ornaments *18, 22, 22, 26,*
    26–27, 41, 63, 74,
    96,.100, 135
  vessels *43*
Grauballe Man 60
Greece
  artistic influence 19
  Celtic invasion *77, 77*–78
  trade 23
Gundestrup Cauldron *34,*
  80–81, *81, 133*

Hadrian's Wall (Britain)
  95, *95, 97*
hairdressing 29
hairstyle *25*
Hallstatt (Austria) *10, 12*
Hannibal 79, 84
harness *46, 60*
heads
  battle trophies *60–61,*
    60–61
  symbolism *25*
helmets *20, 44, 50, 72, 73*

herbal remedies 69
hillforts 16–17, *17*, 76
history 16
Hochdorf (Germany) 39,
  41–42
home life 18–19, 33
honour, women's 35
"honour price" (dowry)
  31
horses, war *38, 49*
household 33
houses
  architecture 17
  Roman-style 93
human sacrifice 57–60,
  59, 131–132
Hungary 75, 80

identity 19, 72–75
Illyrians 73
imports 19–20
industries 13
infidelity 34
Iona (Ireland) *120*
Ireland *101–108, 101–109*
  books *113, 116–117,*
    116–118
  Christianity 107–109,
    112–127, *113–127*
  kings 105–106
  language *9*, 12
  marriage 31
  monasteries 118–123
  religion 134–138
  Romanisation 107
  sacred sites 103–104,
    103–106
  saints 124–126
  scholarship 112–121
  sculpture *106*
Isle of Man language 12
Ita, St 124
Italy
  attacked by Celts
    78–79
  Celtic settlement
    70–75
  monasteries 121
  Roman colonies 89

javelins 48, *50*
jewellery 26, 29
  see also torc neckrings
  Britain 96–97
  bronze *28*
  gold *18, 35, 63, 74*
  silver *37*
Julius Caesar 87–89

kings in Ireland 105–106

"La Tène" art style 20
languages 9, 11–12
  see also literacy;
    writing
  Britain 96
  Danube valley 80
  die out 91
Lepontic Celts 70–71
  language 12
libraries 118
lifestyles 13
  Romanisation 93
Lindow Man *59,* 59–60
literacy in Ireland 115–117
Llyn Cerrig Bach (Anglesey)
  99–100
Lusitanian language 12

Macedonia 77–78
Machas (goddesses)
  136–138
magic
  Irish Christianity 124–126
  women 134
manufacturing industries
  13
Manx language 12
marriage 31, 33–34
medicine 68–69
memory 16, 38
men
  divorce *32*–33
  in stories 143
mercenaries 50–52
metalwork see bronze;
  gold; silver
Mhaol, Grainne 36
Mhor nan Oran,
  Mairi *37*

mining
  gold and silver 14
  salt *1–13*
mirror *32*
mistletoe 68–69
monasteries 95, *113–114,*
  118–123
money 19
  coins 19, *38, 49,* 68,
    76, 87
Morrigan, the Great Queen
  128–129
mother goddess 128–129,
  136
motherhood 31, *31*

names, Celtic 11
nature in art 20
necklace *31*
neckrings *see* "torc"
  neckrings
Nicomedes of Bithynia 78
Numantia (Spain) *82,* 84

occupations 13
"oppida" (hillforts) 16–17,
  17, 76
oral tradition 16
Orkneys 96
otherworld
  beings from 63
  human sacrifice 57–59
  images of 64–67
  life after death 54
  messages from 56

Paris *88*
Patrick, St 124, 126
phallic pillar from
  Euffigneix *64, 64*
Picts 96–98
  Christianity 107
  language *9,* 12
place names 11
plant medicines 69
poetry 16
  Irish 123–124
  women's 36

poets 16, 19, 42, 52,
  53, 140–149
Portugal
  language 12
  military training 49
  Roman conquest 84
  sculptures *17*
  shrines 66
pottery technology 76
Pwyll of Dyfed 138

queens, warrior 24–26

rape 32
religion 54
  see also Christianity;
    druids; otherworld
  Christianity 95
  Gallo-Roman 91,
    91–94
  goddesses 128–138
  Ireland 134–138
  sacred places 62
  women 130–138
Rhiannon 138
Romania 75, 80
Romans
  British rebellion 24–26
  conquer the Celts 83–95
  druids against 55
  Ireland 107
  reclaim Italy 79
  religion 91
Rome, attacks on 74–75,
  78–79
Roscrea Brooch *37*
sacred sites 62, 66,
  66–67
  Ireland *103–104,*
    103–106
sacrifice 68–69, 128
  human 57–60, *59,*
    131–132
saints' magic 124–126
salt *10, 12, 13*
scabbards *40, 47, 100*
scholarship in Ireland
  112–121
Scipio Africanus 84
Scotland 96, 107
  language 12

sculptures
clay figurines 133
Dying Gaul 81
function *17*
goddesses *58, 139*
gods *93, 106*
Ireland *106, 127*
otherworld beings *64–67*
poets *53*
religion *91–94*
torcs *92–94*
warrior *39–40*
warriors *39, 48, 80, 81, 86–87*
sea-urchins 69
Serbia 75, 80
sexuality and fidelity 34
sheep farming 14
shields 48, *49, 50, 71, 73, 100*
shrines 62, *62, 66, 66–67*
Roman 92
silver
mining 14
ornaments *60, 68, 125*
vessel *122*
silver-gilt 80
slavery 16
Slovenia 80
snake symbol *120*
Spain
languages *9,* 12
mining 14
Roman colony 89
Roman conquest 84–85
sculptures *17*
shrines 66, *66, 66–67*
weapons 48
wool and weaving 14
spas 67
spears *44,* 48, *49, 73*
springs *58,* 67
storytelling 140–149
Strettweg 129–130
supernatural 54, 56
Switzerland 121
swords 47, *47,* 48, *50*

Táin, the 142
Taliesin of Rheged 110
Tara (Ireland) *104*
Tara Brooch *35*
technology 76
territory 11, 18
thermal springs 67
Tintagel Castle (Britain) *149*
tombs
chiefs 41–42
excavation 23
Irish 102
warriors 39–42, *44–45*
women 27
torc 22, 26
Britain *22, 26, 96*
Burgundy 27
Germany *41, 63, 81, 81, 135*
Ireland *100*
otherworld 64–66
Portugal *68*
towns 16–17, *17,* 74, 76
trade
Etruscans and Greeks 19, 23
growth of 70
Ireland 107
tradition 16
Trier 94
trophies 60
Turkey 78

urbanisation 74

vanity 8
vase *27*
Vercingetorix of the Arverni 87
vessels *34, 42–43, 75,* 80, *81, 122*
Vettones people *17*
victory trophies 60–61
virgin mothers 126
virginity 33
virtues 8, 38

Vix (Burgundy) 27
votive offerings 67
Wales
children 33
faery 138
war 44–52
see also warriors; weapons
victory trophies 60–61
warriors 38–52
in art *39, 39–40, 48–50*
queens 24–26
sculptures *79–81, 81, 86–87*
tomb *44–45*
torc *79–81, 81*
wealth, personal 23, 70
weapons *20–21, 40, 44–50, 47–48, 71–73,* 100
weaving 14, *14–15*
wells, sacred 67
Welsh language 12
"wicker man" ritual 128
wine pourer *75*
wit 8, 35
witches 134
women 24–37
clothing and jewellery 28–29, *28–29*
divorce 32–33
fairy 138–139
goddesses 128–138
high standing *26–27,* 32
honour 35
independence 36–37
jewellery *26–27*
marriage 31
nuns 118–120
poetry by 36
property 33
religion 130–138
saints 126
in stories 140
wool 14, *14*
words, Celtic 11
writing
introduction 70
Ireland 102, 115

The Celts

First published in the United States of America in 1998 by
RIZZOLI INTERNATIONAL PUBLICATIONS, INC.
300 Park Avenue South, New York, NY 10010

First published in Australia in 1997
by Lansdowne Publishing Pty Ltd
Sydney, Australia

ISBN 0-8478-2105-6
LC 97-76002

Map illustration on page 9 by Dianne Bradley

Publisher: Deborah Nixon
Production Manager: Sally Stokes
Series Editor: Cynthia Blanche
Designer: Robyn Latimer
Project Co-ordinator: Jennifer Coren
Picture Researcher: Jane Lewis
Set in Garamond on QuarkXpress

Printed in Hong Kong by South China Printing Company